FREDERICK DOUGLASS
EARLY AUTOBIOGRAPHICAL
WRITINGS

"His Early Life as a Slave"
and
"What to the Slave is the Fourth of July?"

An excerpt from the complete work: Life and Times of
Frederick Douglass. Written by Himself. His Early Life as a
Slave, His Escape From Bondage, and His Complete History
to the PresentTtime. Along with Frederick Douglass' famous
speech to the citizens of Rochester, New York on July 5, 1852

Introduction by
Professor Ashton Nichols

G.W. Zouck Publishing
Beckleysville, Maryland

This edition is dedicated to
Professor Thomas J. Wilcox
"For teaching us well"

This edition was adapted from a version published in 1893 by
De Wolfe, Fiske & Co. of Boston. New Revised Edition. The
source of Douglass' speech was used with permission from
TeachingAmericanHistory.org. TeachingAmericanHistory.org is
a project of the Ashbrook Center for Public Affairs at Ashland
University.

Sketch of Frederick Douglass by Chloe Mackenzie Probst

ISBN 978-0-9817315-5-1

Printed in the United States of America

CONTENTS

Part 2 – What to the Slave is the Fourth of July?

FREDERICK DOUGLASS AND THE AMERICAN DREAM

F REDERICK Douglass: abolitionist, freethinker, lecturer, and eventual advisor to presidents: who could have imagined that a mixed-race fugitive slave might rise to such a position of prominence in the middle of the nineteenth century? Douglass met many leading Transcendentalist figures during the time that he lectured in Boston and Concord. More importantly, Douglass's life was seen as a perfect embodiment of Transcendentalist ideals. A runaway slave and leader of the Underground Railroad, he was largely self-educated and yet became a best-selling author and counselor to Abraham Lincoln. He began publishing *The North Star*, a widely circulated Abolitionist periodical in 1848, during the same year that the first Women's Rights Convention was held at Seneca Falls. As a lecturer, editor, campaigner for women's rights, and political appointee, Douglass revealed that the power of one person's ideas might become the embodied truth of an entire social movement.

Why was it so difficult for a black man to get his ideas taken seriously in the middle of the nineteenth century? Frederick Douglass was a sort of Martin Luther King, Jr., for the nineteenth century: a public speaker, author, editor, activist and civil-rights campaigner. Douglass's life and his words have often been seen as a living example of the ideals of the New England Transcendentalists and many European abolitionists. As a runaway slave, he was virtually self-educated. His journalism and lecturing connected him to important developing media of the time, giving him a platform and a public. His life and work as an abolitionist came to stand for the power of the moralist and, above all else, power as an individual He broke with both William Lloyd Garrison and John Brown, for example, in favor of the force of his own vision. By the time of his death at the end of the century, he had come to represent the authority of a single soul trying to bring about sweeping social change. He went a long way toward succeeding in the minds of many of those who heard him speak or read his words.

In the course of his long career, Douglass lectured in Boston and Concord and met Emerson, Thoreau, Dr. Channing, and Theodore Parker. Emerson had spoken out in public against slavery for the first time in 1844; by 1851 he attacked the Fugitive Slave Law in front of the people of Concord: "An immoral law makes it a man's duty to break it [. . .] Let us respect the Union to all honest ends. But also respect an older and wider union, the law of Nature and rectitude." Emerson concluded, and many abolitionists came to agree, that any law that might lead to the recapture of runaway slaves needed to be "wiped out of the statute-book; but whilst it stands there, it must be disobeyed." Douglass initially joined these Concordians in support of John Brown; in fact, he became a confidante of Brown up until the time of the Harper's Ferry raid.

His great public power derived initially from the effect of his oratory. Douglass's early speeches dealt mainly with his own experiences; some refused to believe that he had been a slave. Those who heard him speak reported the dramatic power of the oratory. He described slave-owners beating slaves of every sort, a young girl's head "covered with festering sores," and the practice of breeding slaves like prized animals. Some of these details were news at the time to Northerners. "I have often been awakened at the dawn of day by the most heart-rending shrieks of an old aunt of mine, whom [Mr. Plummer] used to tie up to a joist, and whip upon her naked back till she was literally covered with blood. No words, no tears, no prayers from his gory victim seemed to move his iron heart from its bloody purpose. The louder she screamed, the harder he whipped; and where the blood ran fastest, there he whipped longest. He would whip her to make her scream, and whip her to make her hush; and not until overcome by fatigue, would he cease to swing the blood-clotted cowskin" (*Narrative* 1845). He could even use humor to good effect in such a work, as in his retelling of the moment when he "broke the slave breaker" named Edward Covey by fighting back, an unheard of response at the time. Likewise, he offered a laughable imitation of clergy in their pulpits promising slaves that God would be angered if they dared to disobey their owners and masters.

From his birth into slavery until his death as an internationally famous figure, Douglass fought tirelessly for the rights of black Americans, and he linked those rights to the wider rights of all human beings. Born a slave on the Eastern Shore of Maryland in 1818, he was the son of a white man and a slave woman, a mother whom he saw only a few times in his life. He escaped once and was recaptured, an event he recorded as one of his most terrible experiences, freedom achieved and then taken away. He escaped for good when he was twenty by impersonating a sailor, but in certain places he was still a fugitive for decades until the Civil War ended. He had met the free black woman Anna Murray while he was still enslaved; they married and moved north to Massachusetts to begin a family. He soon lectured for the Massachusetts Anti-Slavery Society and met William Lloyd Garrison. His career as a public speaker and writer flourished; who but a former slave could speak or write with this accuracy and conviction? Douglass began a related career in 1847 with the first publication of *The North Star*, a weekly to rival Garrison's *Liberator*; Douglass's masthead motto was: "Right is of no sex -- Truth is of no color -- God is the Father of us all, and we are all Brethren," a motto which echoed the famous British abolitionist motto, "Am I not a Man and a Brother?" In 1848 he attended the first convention for women's rights held at Seneca Falls, where he linked the struggles of slaves directly to the struggles of oppressed women, a full half of the human population. Douglass traveled to England where he claimed to have felt fully free for the first time, and where he came to link the rights of slaves to the rights of oppressed people of all kinds. His lectures came to support women, Irish home rule, and the temperance movement. He returned to England later, when he feared for his own safety, worried that his links to John Brown's raid and execution might get him in personal trouble with the authorities.

By the time of the Civil War, Douglass was enough of a public figure to be called to the White House for meetings with Lincoln. Lincoln called him "my friend Douglass." Douglass's influence also helped him to become a recruiter for black soldiers eventually totaling two companies, including two sons of Douglass. He also went on to meet with Andrew Johnson after the war to discuss the rights of formers slaves and the complex issues surrounding Reconstruction. After the end of the Civil War, Douglass actively supported those constitutional amendments that made equal rights into a matter of law. The issue was by no means settled, however. He consistently lamented the lack of real opportunity for black people and the continuing segregationist separation of the races. He claimed that racism was not merely "a southern problem." After the Civil War, he wrote, "Did John

Brown fail? [. . .] John Brown began the war that ended American slavery and made this a free Republic [. . .] His zeal in the cause of my race was far greater than mine." His own life was not always free from racial controversy. Late in life, after the death of his first wife, Douglass married his white former secretary. He silenced critics of this marriage by saying that his mother's race was honored by his first marriage, his father's race by his second marriage.

How was Douglass able to break down the barriers that separated him from white society and become such a powerful and influential individual? The legacy of Douglass was widespread and powerful in America and beyond. His writings were bestsellers, and he spoke out publicly until the end of his life. *Narrative of the Life of Frederick Douglass, An American Slave, Written by Himself* (1845) was his first book. *My Bondage, My Freedom* (1855) described his first trip to England and added "What to the Slave is the Fourth of July?": "The blessings in which you, this day, rejoice, are not enjoyed in common. The rich inheritance of justice, liberty, prosperity and independence, bequeathed by your fathers, is shared by you, not by me. The sunlight that brought life and healing to you, has brought stripes and death to me. This Fourth [of] July is yours, not mine. You may rejoice, I must mourn. To drag a man in fetters into the grand illuminated temple of liberty, and call upon him to join you in joyous anthems, were inhuman mockery and sacrilegious irony." In 1881, he published the third of his autobiographical volumes, *Life and Times of Frederick Douglass*. Each subsequent volume added more details and more candor to the story.

Many, like the poet Paul Laurence Dunbar, celebrated Douglass: "To sin and crime he gave their proper hue, / And hurled at evil what was evil's due." Douglass's "What to the Slave is the Fourth of July?" has been compared to Martin Luther King's "I Have a Dream" speech, not in terms of optimism, but rather in recognition of, in King's words, the "withering injustice" at the heart of American democracy and a continuing "lonely island of poverty in the midst of a vast ocean of material prosperity." Douglass, as the work you hold in your hands powerfully proves, wanted to make the grand promises of America available to all of America's citizens. Barack Obama may be in the White House, but the work of Douglass's legacy clearly continues.

———————————

Ashton Nichols is the John J. Curley '60 and Ann ConserCurley '63 Professor of Liberal Arts at Dickinson College in Carlisle, Pennsylvania. His recorded lecture series, *Emerson, Thoreau, and American Transcendentalism*, has recently appeared as part of the "Great Courses" program of The Teaching Company. He is the author of *The Poetics of Epiphany* and *The Revolutionary "I"* and editor of *Romantic Natural Histories.* Ashton Nichol's newest book is titled *"Beyond Romantic Ecocriticism:Toward Urbanatural Roosting"* and is published as part of the "Nineteenth Century Major Lives and Letters"series by Palgrave Macmillan.

MY LIFE AS A SLAVE.

By Frederick Douglass

Chapter I.

AUTHOR'S BIRTH.

Author's place of birth—Description of country—Its inhabitants— Genealogical trees—Method of counting time in slave districts— Date of author's birth—Names of grandparents—Their cabin— Home with them—Slave practice of separating mothers from their children—Author's recollections of his mother—Who was his father?

I N Talbot County, Eastern Shore, State of Maryland, near Easton, the county town, there is a small district of country, thinly populated, and remarkable for nothing that I know of more than for the worn-out, sandy, desert- like appearance of its soil, the general dilapidation of its farms and fences, the indigent and spiritless character of its inhabitants, and the prevalence of ague and fever. It was in this dull, flat, and unthrifty district or neighborhood, bordered by the Choptank river, among the laziest and muddiest of streams, surrounded by a white population of the lowest order, indolent and drunken to a proverb, and among slaves who, in point of ignorance and indolence, were fully in accord with their surroundings, that I, without any fault of my own, was born, and spent the first years of my childhood.

The reader must not expect me to say much of my family. Genealogical trees did not flourish among slaves. A person of some consequence in civilized society, sometimes designated as father, was literally unknown to slave law and to slave practice. I never met with a slave in that part of the country who could tell me with any certainty how old he was. Few at that time knew anything of the months of the year or of the days of the month. They measured the ages of their children by spring-time, winter-time, harvest-time, planting-time, and the like. Masters allowed no questions concerning their ages to be put to them by slaves. Such questions were regarded by the masters as evidence of an impudent curiosity. From certain events, however, the dates of which I have since learned, I suppose myself to have been born in February, 1817.

My first experience of life, as I now remember it, and I remember it but hazily, began in the family of my grand mother and grandfather, Betsey and Isaac Bailey. They were considered old settlers in the neighborhood, and from certain circumstances I infer that my grandmother, especially, was held in high esteem, far higher than was the lot of most colored persons in that region. She was a good nurse, and a capital hand at making nets used for catching shad and herring, and was, withal, somewhat famous as a fisherwoman. I have known her to be in the water waist deep, for hours, seine-hauling. She was a gardener as well as a fisherwoman, and remarkable for her success in keeping her seedling sweet potatoes through the months of winter, and easily got the reputation of being born to " good luck." In planting-time Grand mother Betsey was sent for in all directions, simply to place the seedling potatoes in the hills or drills; for superstition had it that her touch was needed to make them grow. This reputation was full of advantage to her and her grandchildren, for a good crop, after her planting for the neighbors, brought her a share of the harvest.

Whether because she was too old for field service, or because she had so faithfully discharged the duties of her station in early life, I know not, but she enjoyed the high privilege of living in a cabin separate from the quarters, having imposed upon her only the charge of the young children and the burden of her own support. She esteemed it great good fortune to live so, and took, much comfort in having the children. The practice of separating mothers from their children and hiring them out at distances too great to admit of their meeting, save at long intervals, was a marked feature of the cruelty and barbarity of the slave system; but it was in harmony with the grand aim of that system, which always and everywhere sought to reduce man to a level with the brute. It had no interest in recognizing or preserving any of the ties that bind families together or to their homes.

My grandmother's five daughters were hired out in this way, and my only recollections of my own mother are of a few hasty visits made in the night on foot, after the daily tasks were over, and when she was under the necessity of returning in time to respond to the driver's call to the field in the early morning. These little glimpses of my mother, obtained under such circumstances and against such odds, meager as they were, are ineffaceably stamped upon my memory. She was tall and finely proportioned, of dark, glossy complexion, with regular features, and amongst the slaves was remarkably sedate and dignified. There is, in "Prichard's Natural History of Man," the head of a figure, on page 157, the features of which so resemble my mother that I often recur to it with something of the feelings which I suppose others experience when looking upon the likenesses of their own dear departed ones.

Of my father I know nothing. Slavery had no recognition of fathers, as none of families. That the mother was a slave was enough for its deadly purpose. By its law the child followed the condition of its mother. The father might be a freeman and the child a slave. The father might be a white man, glorying in the purity of his Anglo-Saxon blood, and the child ranked with the blackest slaves. Father he might be, and not be husband, and could sell his own child without incurring reproach, if in its veins coursed one drop of African blood.

Chapter II.

REMOVAL FROM GRANDMOTHER'S.

Author's early home—Its charms—Author's ignorance of "old master"—His gradual perception of the truth concerning him—His relations to Col. Edward Lloyd—Author's removal to "old master's" home—His journey thence—His separation from his grand-mother—His grief.

L IVING thus with my grandmother, whose kindness and love stood in place of my mother's, it was some time before I knew myself to be a slave. I knew many other things before I knew that. Her little cabin had to me the attractions of a palace. Its fence-railed floor—which was equally floor and bedstead—up stairs, and its clay floor down stairs, its dirt and straw chimney, and windowless sides, and that most curious piece of workmanship, the ladder stairway, and the hole so strangely dug in front of the fire-place, beneath which grandmamma placed her sweet potatoes, to keep them from frost in winter, were full of interest to my childish observation. The squirrels, as they skipped the fences, climbed the trees, or gathered their nuts, were an unceasing delight to me. There, too, right at the side of the hut, stood the old well, with its stately and skyward-pointing beam, so aptly placed between the limbs of what had once been a tree, and so nicely balanced, that I could move it up and down with only one hand, and could get a drink myself without calling for help. Nor were these all the attractions of the place. At a little distance stood Mr. Lee's mill, where the people came in large numbers to get their corn ground. I can never tell the many things thought and felt, as I sat on the bank and watched that mill, and the turning of its ponderous wheel. The mill-pond, too, had its charms, and with my pin-hook and thread line, I could get amusing nibbles if I could catch no fish.

It was not long, however, before I began to learn the sad fact that this house of my childhood belonged not to my dear old grandmother, but to some one I had never seen, and who lived a great distance off. I learned, too, the sadder fact, that not only the home and lot, but that grandmother herself and all the little children around, her belonged to a mysterious personage, called by grand mother, with every mark of reverence, "Old Master." Thus early did clouds and shadows begin to fall upon my path.

I learned that this old master, whose name seemed ever to be mentioned with fear and shuddering, only allowed the little children to live with grandmother for a limited time, and that as soon as they were big enough they were promptly taken away to live with the said old master. These were distressing revelations, indeed. My grandmother was all the world to me, and the thought of being separated from her was a most unwelcome suggestion to my affections and hopes. This mysterious old master was really a man of some consequence. He owned several farms in Tuckahoe, was the chief clerk and butler on the home plantation of Colonel Lloyd, had overseers as well as slaves on his own farms, and gave directions to the overseers on the farms owned by Colonel Lloyd. Captain Aaron Anthony, for such is the name and title of my old master, lived on Colonel Lloyd's plantation, which was situated on the Wye river, and which was one of the largest, most fertile, and best appointed n the State.

About this plantation and this old master I was most eager to know everything which could be known; and, unhappily for me, all the information I could get concerning him increased my dread of being separated from my grandmother and grandfather. I wished that it was possible for me to remain small all my life, knowing that the sooner I grew large the shorter would be my time to remain with them. Everything about the cabin became doubly dear and I was sure that there could be no other spot on earth equal to it. But the time came when I must go, and my grandmother, knowing my fears, and in pity for them, kindly kept me ignorant of the dreaded moment up to the morning (a beautiful summer morning) when we were to start; and, indeed, during the whole journey, which, child as I was, I remember as well as if it were yesterday, she kept the unwelcome truth hidden from me. The distance from Tuckahoe to Colonel Lloyd's, where my old master lived, was full twelve miles, and the walk was quite a severe test of the endurance of my young legs. The journey would have proved too severe for me, but that my dear old grandmother (blessings on her memory) afforded occasional relief by "toteing" me on her shoulder. Advanced in years as she was, as was evident from the more than one gray hair which peeped from between the ample and graceful folds of her newly and smoothly-ironed bandana turban, grandmother was yet a woman of power and spirit. She was remarkably Straight in figure, and elastic and muscular in movement. I seemed hardly to be a burden to her. She would have "toted" me farther, but I felt myself too much of a man to allow it. Yet while I walked I was not independent of her. She often found me holding her skirts lest something should come out of the woods and eat me up. Several old logs and stumps imposed upon me, and got themselves taken for enormous animals. I could plainly see their legs, eyes, ears, and teeth, till I got close enough to see that the eyes were knots, washed white with rain, and the legs were broken limbs, and the ears and teeth only such because of the point from which they were seen.

As the day advanced the heat increased, and it was not until the afternoon that we reached the much-dreaded end of the journey. Here I found myself in the midst of a group of children of all sizes and of many colors, black, brown, copper-colored, and nearly white. 1 had not before seen so many children. As a new-comer I was an object of special interest. After laughing and yelling around me and playing all sorts of wild tricks, they asked me to go out and play with them. This I refused to do. Grandmamma looked sad, and I could not help feeling that our being there boded no good to me. She was soon to lose another object of affection, as she had lost many before. Affectionately patting me on the head, she told me to be a good boy and go out to play with the children. They are "kin to you," she said, " go and play with them." She pointed out to me my brother Perry, and my sisters, Sarah and Eliza. I had never seen them before, and though I had sometimes heard of them and felt a curious interest in them, I really did not understand what they were to me or I to them. Brothers and sisters we were by blood, but slavery had made us strangers. They were already initiated into the mysteries of old master's domicile, and they seemed to look upon me with a certain degree of compassion. I really wanted to play with them, but they were strangers to me, and I was full of fear that my grandmother might leave for home without taking me with her. Entreated to do so, however, and that, too, by my dear grandmother, I went to the back part of the house to play with them and the other children. Play, however, I did not, but stood with my back against the wall witnessing the playing of the others. At last, while standing there, one of the children, who had been in the kitchen, ran up to me in a sort of roguish glee, exclaiming, "Fed, Fed, grandmamma gone!" I could not believe it. Yet, fearing the worst, I ran into the kitchen to see for myself, and lo! she was indeed gone, and was now far away, and "clean" out of sight. I need not tell all that happened now. Almost heart-broken at the discovery, I fell upon the ground and wept a boy's bitter tears, refusing to be comforted. My brother gave me peaches and pears to quiet me, but I promptly threw them on the ground. I had never been deceived before and something of resentment mingled with my grief at parting with my grand-mother.

It was now late in the afternoon. The day had been an exciting and wearisome one, and I know not where, but I suppose I sobbed myself to sleep; and its balm was never more welcome to any wounded soul than to mine. The reader may be surprised that I relate so minutely an incident apparently so trivial, and which must have occurred when I was less than seven years old; but, as I wish to give a faithful history of my experience in slavery, I cannot withhold a circumstance which at the time affected me so deeply, and which I still remember so vividly. Besides, this was my first introduction to the realities of the slave system.

Chapter III.

TROUBLES OF CHILDHOOD.

Col. Lloyd's plantation—Aunt Katy—Her cruelty and ill-nature— Capt. Anthony's partiality to Aunt Katy—Allowance of food— Author's hunger—Unexpected rescue by his mother—The reproof of Aunt Katy—Sleep—A slave-mother's love—Author's inheritance —His mother's acquirements—Her death.

ONCE established on the home plantation of Col. Lloyd—I was with the children there, left to the tender mercies of Aunt Katy, a slave woman, who was to my master what he was to Col. Lloyd. Disposing of us in classes or sizes, he left to Aunt Katy all the minor details concerning our management. She was a woman who never allowed herself to act greatly within the limits of delegated power, no matter how broad that authority might be. Ambitious of old master's favor, ill-tempered and cruel by nature, she found in her present position an ample field for the exercise of her ill-omened qualities. She had a strong hold upon old master, for she was a first-rate cook, and very industrious. She was therefore greatly favored by him—and as one mark of his favor she was the only mother who was permitted to retain her children around her, and even to these, her own children, she was often fiendish in her brutality. Cruel, however, as she sometimes was to her own children, she was not destitute of maternal feeling, and in her instinct to satisfy their demands for food she was often guilty of starving me and the other children. Want of food was my chief trouble during my first summer here. Captain Anthony, instead of allowing a given quantity of food to each slave, committed the allowance for all to Aunt Katy, to be divided by her, after cooking, amongst us. The allowance consisted of coarse corn-meal, not very abundant, and which, by passing through Aunt Katy's hands, became more slender still for some of us. I have often been so pinched with hunger as to dispute with old " Nep," the dog, for the crumbs which fell from the kitchen table. Many times have I followed, with eager step, the waiting-girl when she shook the table-cloth, to get the crumbs and small bones flung out for the dogs and cats. It was a great thing to have the privilege of dipping a piece of bread into the water in which meat had been boiled, and the skin taken from the rusty bacon was a positive luxury. With this description of the domestic arrangements of my new home, I may here recount a circumstance which is deeply impressed on my memory, as affording a bright gleam of a slave-mother's love, and the earnestness of a mother's care. I had offended Aunt Katy. I do not remember in what way, for my offences were numerous in that quarter, greatly depending upon her moods as to their heinousness, and she had adopted her usual mode of punishing me : namely, making me go all day without food. For the first hour or two after dinner time, I succeeded pretty well in keeping up my spirits; but as the day wore away, I found it quite impossible to do so any longer. Sundown came, but no bread; and in its stead came the threat from Aunt Katy, with a scowl well-suited to its terrible import, that she would starve the life out of me. Brandishing her knife, she chopped off the heavy slices of bread for the other children, and put the loaf away; muttering all the while her savage designs upon myself. Against this disappointment, for I was expecting that her heart would relent at last, I made an extra effort to maintain my dignity, but when I saw the other children around me with satisfied faces, I could stand it no longer. I went out behind the kitchen wall and cried like a line fellow. When wearied with this, I returned to the kitchen, sat by the fire and brooded over my hard lot. I was too hungry to sleep. While I sat in the corner, I caught sight of an ear of Indian corn upon an upper shelf. I watched my chance and got it; and shelling off a few grains, I put it back again. These grains 1 quickly put into the hot ashes to roast. I did this at the risk of getting a brutal thumping, for Aunt Katy could beat as well as starve me. My corn was not long in roasting, and I eagerly pulled it from the ashes, and placed it upon a stool in a clever little pile. I began to help myself, when who but my own dear mother should come in. The scene which followed is beyond my power to describe. The friendless and hungry boy, in his extremest need, found himself in the strong, protecting arms of his mother. I have before spoken of my mother's dignified and impressive manner. I shall never forget the indescribable expression of her countenance when I told her that Aunt Katy had said she would starve the life out of me. There was deep and tender pity in her glance at me, and, at the same moment, a fiery indignation at Aunt Katy, and while she took the corn from me, and gave in its stead a large ginger-cake, she read Aunt Katy a lecture which was never forgotten. That night I learned as I had never learned before, that I was not only a child, but somebody's child. I was grander upon my mother's knee than a king upon his throne. But my triumph was short. I dropped off to sleep, and waked in the morning to find my mother gone and myself at the mercy again of the virago in my master's kitchen, whose fiery wrath was my constant dread.

My mother had walked twelve miles to see me, and had the same distance to travel over again before the morning sunrise. I do not remember ever seeing her again. Her death soon ended the little communication that had existed between us, and with it, I believe, a life full of weariness and heartfelt sorrow. To me it has ever been a grief that I knew my mother so little, and have so few of her words treasured in my remembrance. I have since learned that she was the only one of all the colored people of Tuckahoe who could read. How she acquired this knowledge I know not, for Tuckahoe was the last place in the world where she would have been likely to find facilities for learning. I can therefore fondly and proudly ascribe to her an earnest love of knowledge. That in any slave State a field-hand should learn to read is remarkable, but the achievement of my mother, considering the place and circumstances, was very extraordinary. In view of this fact, I am happy to attribute any love of letters I may have, not to my presumed Anglo-Saxon paternity, but to the native genius of my sable, unprotected, and uncultivated mother—a woman who belonged to a race whose mental endowments are still disparaged and despised.

Chapter IV.

A GENERAL SURVEY OF THE SLAVE PLANTATION.

Home Plantation of Colonel Lloyd—Its Isolation—Its Industries— The Slave Rule—Power of Overseers—Author Finds sonic Enjoyment—Natural Scenery—Sloop "Sally Lloyd" —Wind Mill—Slave-Quarter—"Old Master's" House—Stables, Store Houses, etc., etc. —The Great House—Its Surroundings—Lloyd—Burial-Place—Superstition of Slaves—Colonel Lloyd's Wealth—Negro Politeness —Doctor Copper—Captain Anthony—His Family—Master Daniel Lloyd—His Brothers—Social Etiquette.

I T was generally supposed that slavery in the State of Maryland existed in its mildest form, and that it was totally divested of those harsh and terrible peculiarities which characterized the slave system in the Southern and South- Western States of the American Union. The ground of this opinion was the contiguity of the free States, and the influence of their moral, religious, and humane sentiments. Public opinion was, indeed, a measurable restraint upon the cruelty and barbarity of masters, overseers, and slave-drivers, whenever and wherever it could reach them; but there were certain secluded and out-of-the-way places, even in the State of Maryland, fifty years ago, seldom visited by a single ray of healthy public sentiment, where slavery, wrapt in its own congenial darkness, could and did develop all its malign and shocking characteristics, where it could he indecent without shame, cruel without shuddering, and murderous without apprehension or fear of exposure or punishment. Just such a secluded, dark, and out-of-the-way place was the home plantation of Colonel Edward Lloyd, in Talbot county, eastern shore of Maryland. It was far away. from all the great thoroughfares of travel and commerce, and proximate to no town or village. There was neither school-house nor town-house in its neighborhood. The school-house was unnecessary, for there were no children to go to school. The children and grandchildren of Col. Lloyd were taught in the house by a private tutor (a Mr. Page from Greenfield, Massachusetts, a tall, gaunt sapling of a man, remarkably dignified, thoughtful, and reticent, and who did not speak a dozen words to a slave in a whole year). The overseer's children went off somewhere in the State to school, and therefore could bring no foreign or dangerous influence from abroad to embarrass the natural operation of the slave system of the place. Here, not even the commonest mechanics, from whom there might have been an occasional outburst of honest and telling indignation at cruelty and wrong on other plantations, were white men. Its whole public was made up of and divided into three classes, slaveholders, slaves, and overseers. Its blacksmiths, wheelwrights, shoemakers, weavers, and coopers were slaves. Not even commerce, selfish and indifferent to moral considerations as it usually is, was permitted within its secluded precincts. Whether with a view of guarding against the escape of its secrets, I know not, but it is a fact, that every leaf and grain of the products of (his plantation and those of the neighboring farms belonging to Col. Lloyd were transported to Baltimore in his own vessels, every man and boy on board of which, except the captain, were owned by him as his property. In return, everything brought to the plantation came through the same channel. To make this isolation more apparent, it may be stated that the estates adjoining Col. Lloyds were owned and occupied by friends of his, who were as deeply interested as himself in maintaining the slave system in all its rigor. These were the Tilgmans, the Goldboroughs, the Lockermans, the Pacas, the Skinners, Gibsons, and others of lesser affluence and standing.

Public opinion in such, a quarter, the reader must see, was not likely to be very efficient in protecting the slave from cruelty. To be a restraint upon abuses of this nature, opinion must emanate from humane and virtuous communities, and to no such opinion or influence was Col. Lloyd's plantation exposed. It was a little nation by itself, having its own language, its own rules, regulations, and customs. The troubles and controversies arising here were not settled by the civil power of the State. The overseer was the important dignitary. He was generally accuser, judge, jury, advocate, and executioner. The criminal was always dumb, and no slave was allowed to testify other than against his brother slave.

There were, of course, no conflicting rights of property, for all the people were the property of one man, and they could themselves own no property. Religion and politics were largely excluded. One class of the population was too high to be reached by the common preacher, and the other class was too low in condition and ignorance to be much cared for by religious teachers, and yet some religious ideas did enter this dark corner.

This, however, is not the only view which the place presented. Though civilization was, in many respects, shut out, nature could not be. Though separated from the rest of the world, though public opinion, as I have said, could seldom penetrate its dark domain, though the whole place was stamped with its own peculiar iron-like individuality, and though crimes, high-handed and atrocious, could be committed there with strange and shocking impunity, it was, to outward seeming, a most strikingly interesting place, full of life, activity, and spirit, and presented a very favorable contrast to the indolent monotony and languor of Tuckahoe. It resembled, in some respects, descriptions I have since read of the old baronial domains of Europe. Keen as was my regret and great as was my sorrow at leaving my old home, I was not long in adapting myself to this my new one. A man's troubles are always half disposed of when he finds endurance the only alternative. I found myself here, there was no getting away, and naught remained for me but to make the best of it. Here were plenty of children to play with and plenty of pleasant resorts for boys of my age and older. The little tendrils of affection, so rudely broken from the darling objects in and around my grandmother's home, gradually began to extend and twine themselves around the new surroundings. Here, for the first time, I saw a large windmill, with its wide-sweeping white wings, a commanding object to a child's eye. This was situated on what was called Long Point— a tract of land dividing Miles river from the Wye. I spent many hours here watching the wings of this wondrous mill. In the river, or what was called the "Swash," at a short distance from the shore, quietly lying at anchor, with her small row boat dancing at her stern, was a large sloop, the Sally Lloyd, called by that name in honor of the favorite daughter of the Colonel. These two objects, the sloop and mill, awakened as I remember, thoughts, ideas, and wondering. Then here were a great many houses, human habitations full of the mysteries of life at every stage of it. There was the little red house up the road, occupied by Mr.

Seveir, the overseer. A little nearer to my old master's stood a long, low, rough building literally alive with slaves of all ages, sexes, conditions, sizes, and colors. This was called the long quarter. Perched upon a hill east of our house, was a tall, dilapidated old brick building, the architectural dimensions of which proclaimed its creation for a different purpose, now occupied by slaves, in a similar manner to the long quarters. Besides these, there were numerous other slave houses and huts scattered around in the neighborhood, every nook and corner of which were completely occupied.

Old master's house, a long brick building, plain but substantial, was centrally located, and was an independent establishment. Besides these houses there were barns, stables, store-houses, tobacco-houses, blacksmith shops, wheelwright shops, cooper shops; but above all there stood the grandest building my young eyes had ever beheld, called by every one on the plantation the *great* house. This was occupied by Col. Lloyd and his family. It was surrounded by numerous and variously-shaped out-buildings. There were kitchens, wash-houses, dairies, summer-houses, green-houses, hen-houses, turkey-houses, pigeon-houses, and arbors of many sizes and devices, all neatly painted or whitewashed, interspersed with grand old trees, ornamental and primitive, which afforded delightful shade in summer and imparted to the scene a high degree of stately beauty. The *great* house itself was a large white wooden building with wings on three sides of it. In front, extending the entire length of the building and supported by a long range of columns, was a broad portico, which gave to the Colonel's home an air of great dignity and grandeur. It was a treat to my young and gradually opening mind to behold this elaborate exhibition of wealth, power and beauty.

The carriage entrance to the house was by a large gate more than a quarter of a mile distant. The intermediate space was a beautiful lawn, very neatly kept and tended. It, was dotted thickly over with trees and flowers. The road or lane from the gate to the great house was richly paved with white pebbles from the beach and in its course formed a complete circle around the lawn. Outside this select enclosure were parks, as about the residences of the English nobility, where rabbits, deer, and other wild game might be seen peering and playing about, with " none to molest them or make them afraid." The tops of the stately poplars were often covered with red-winged blackbirds, making all nature vocal with the joyous life and beauty of their wild, warbling notes. These all belonged to me as well as to Col. Edward Lloyd, and, whether they did or not, I greatly enjoyed them. Not far from the great house were the stately mansions of the dead Lloyds—a place of somber aspect. Vast tombs, embowered beneath the weeping willow and the fir tree, told of the generations of the family, as well as of their wealth. Superstition was rife among the slaves about this family burying-ground. Strange sights had been seen there by some of. the older slaves, and I was often compelled to hear stories of shrouded ghosts, riding on great black horses, and of balls of fire which had been seen to fly there at midnight, and of startling and dreadful sounds that had been repeatedly heard. Slaves knew enough of the Orthodox theology of the time, to consign all bad slaveholders to hell, and they often fancied such persons wishing themselves back again to wield the lash. Tales of sights and sounds strange and terrible, connected with the huge black tombs, were a great security to the grounds about them, for few of the slaves had the courage to approach them during the day time. It was a dark, gloomy, and forbidding place, and it was difficult to feel that the spirits of the sleeping dust there deposited reigned with the blest in the realms of eternal peace.

At Lloyd's, was transacted the business of twenty or thirty different farms, which, with the slaves upon them, numbering, in all, not less than a thousand, all belonged to Col. Lloyd. Each farm was under the management of an overseer, whose word was law.

Mr. Lloyd was, at this time, very rich. His slaves alone, numbering as I have said not less than a thousand, were an immense fortune, and though scarcely a month passed without the sale to the Georgia traders, of one or more lots, there was no apparent diminution in the number of his human stock. The selling of any to the State of Georgia was a sore and mournful event to those left behind, as well as to the victims themselves.

The reader has already been informed of the handi-crafts carried on here by the slaves. " Uncle " Toney was the blacksmith, " Uncle " Harry the Cartwright, and "Uncle"Abel was the shoemaker, and these had assistants in their several departments. These mechanics were called " Uncles" by all the younger slaves, not because they really sustained that relationship to any, but according to plantation etiquette, as a mark of respect, due from the younger to the older slaves. Strange and even ridiculous as it may seem, among a people so uncultivated and with so many stern trials to look in the face, there is not to be found among any people a more rigid enforcement of the law of respect to elders than is maintained among them. I set this down as partly constitutional with the colored race and partly conventional. There is no better material in the world for making a gentleman than is fur-nished in the African.

Among other slave notabilities, I found here one called by everybody, white and colored, " Uncle " Isaac Copper.

It was seldom that a slave, however venerable, was honored with a surname in Maryland, and so completely has the south shaped the manners of the north in this respect that their right to such honor is tardily admitted even now. It goes sadly against the grain to address and treat a negro as one would address and treat a white man. But once in a while, even in a slave state, a negro had a surname fastened to him by common consent. This was the case with " Uncle " Isaac Copper. When the " Uncle " was dropped, he was called Doctor Copper. He was both our Doctor of Medicine and our Doctor of Divinity. Where he took his degree I am unable to say, but he was too well established in his profession to permit question as to his native skill or attainments. One qualification he certainly had. He was a confirmed cripple, wholly unable to work, and was worth nothing for sale in the market. Though lame, he was no sluggard. He made his crutches do him good service, and was always on the alert looking up the sick, and such as were supposed to need his aid and counsel. His remedial prescriptions embraced four articles. For diseases of the body, epsom salts and castor oil; for those of the soul, the " Lord's prayer," and a few stout hickory switches.

I was, with twenty or thirty other children, early sent to Doctor Isaac Copper, to learn the Lord's prayer. The old man was seated on a huge three-legged oaken stool, armed with several large hickory switches, and from the point where he sat, lame as he was, he could reach every boy in the room. After our standing a while to learn what was expected of us, he commanded us to kneel down. This done, he told us to say everything he said. "Our Father"—this we repeated after him with promptness and uniformity— "who art in Heaven," was less promptly and uniformly repeated, and the old gentleman paused in the prayer to give us a short lecture, and to use his switches on our backs.

Everybody in the South seemed to want the privilege of whipping somebody else. Uncle Isaac, though a good old man, shared the common passion of his time and country. I cannot say I was much edified by attendance upon his ministry. There was in my mind, even at that time, something a little inconsistent and laughable in the blending of prayer with punishment.

I was not long in my now home before I found that the dread I had conceived of Captain Anthony was in a meas-ure groundless. Instead of leaping out from some hiding-place and destroying me, he hardly seemed to notice my presence. He probably thought as little of my arrival there as of an additional pig to his stock. He was the chief agent of his employer. The overseers of all the farms composing the Lloyd estate were in some sort under him. The Colonel himself' seldom addressed an overseer, or allowed himself to be addressed by one. To Captain Anthony, therefore, was committed the headship of all the farms. He carried the keys of all the store-houses, weighed and measured the allowances of each slave, at the end of each month; superintended the storing of all goods brought to the store-house; dealt out the raw material to the different handicraftsmen; shipped the grain, tobacco, and all other saleable produce of the numerous farms to Baltimore, and had a general oversight of all the workshops of the place. In addition to all this he was frequently called abroad to Easton and elsewhere in the discharge of his numerous duties as chief agent of the estate.

The family of Captain Anthony consisted of two sons —Andrew and Richard, and his daughter Lucretia and her newly-married husband, Captain Thomas Auld. In the kitchen were Aunt Katy, Aunt Esther, and ten or a dozen children, most of them older than myself. Captain Anthony was not considered a rich slave-holder, though he was pretty well off in the world. He owned about thirty slaves and three farms in the Tuckahoe district. The more valuable part of his property was in slaves, of whom he sold.one every year, which brought him in seven or eight hundred dollars, besides his yearly salary and other revenue from his lands.

I have been often asked, during the earlier part of my free life at the North, how I happened to have so little of the slave accent in my speech. The mystery is in some measure explained by my association with Daniel Lloyd, the youngest son of Col. Edward Lloyd. The law of compensation holds here as well as elsewhere. While this lad could not associate with ignorance without sharing its shade, he could not give his black playmates his company without giving them his superior intelligence as well. Without knowing this, or caring about it at the time, I, for some cause or other, was attracted to him, and was much his companion.

I had little to do with the older brothers of Daniel— Edward and Murray. They were grown up and were fine-looking men. Edward was especially esteemed by the slave children, and by me among the rest—not that he ever said anything to us or for us which could by called particularly kind. It was enough for us that he never looked or acted scornfully toward us. The idea of rank and station was rigidly maintained on this estate. The family of Captain Anthony never visited the great house, and the Lloyds never came to our house. Equal non-intercourse was observed between Captain Anthony's family and the family of Mr. Seveir, the overseer.

Such, kind readers, was the community and such the place in which my earliest and most lasting impressions of the workings of slavery were received, of which impressions you will learn more in the after coming chapters of this book.

31

Chapter V.

A SLAVEHOLDER'S CHARACTER.

Increasing acquaintance with old Master—Evils of unresisted passion —Apparent tenderness—A man of trouble— Custom of muttering to himself—Brutal outrage—A drunken overseer—Slaveholder's impatience—Wisdom of appeal—A base and selfish attempt to break up a courtship.

ALTHOUGH my old master, Captain Anthony, gave me, at 'the first of my coming to him from my grandmother's, very little attention, and although that little was of a remarkably mild and gentle description, a few months only were sufficient to convince me that mildness and gentleness were not the prevailing or governing traits of his character. These excellent qualities were displayed only occasionally. He could, when it suited him, appear to be literally insensible to the claims of humanity. He could not only be deaf to the appeals of the helpless against the aggressor, but he could himself commit outrages deep, dark, and nameless. Yet he was not by nature worse than other men. Had he been brought up in a free state, surrounded by the full restraints of civilized society—restraints which are necessary to the freedom of all its members, alike and equally, Capt. Anthony might have been as humane a man as are members of such society generally. A man's character always takes its hue, more or less, from the form and color of things about him. The slaveholder, as well as the slave, was the victim of the slave system. Under the whole heavens there could be no relation more unfavorable to the development of honorable character than that sustained by the slaveholder to the slave. Reason is imprisoned here, and passions run wild. Could the reader have seen Captain Anthony gently leading me by the hand, as he sometimes did, patting me on the head, speaking to me in soft, caressing tones, and calling me his little Indian boy, he would have deemed him a kind-hearted old man, and really almost fatherly to the slave boy. But the pleasant moods of a slaveholder are transient and fitful. They neither come often nor remain long. The temper of the old man was subject to special trials; but since these trials were never borne patiently, they added little to his natural stock of patience. Aside from his troubles with his slaves and those of Mr. Lloyd, he made the impression upon me of being an unhappy man. Even to my child's eye he wore a troubled and at times a haggard aspect. His strange movements excited my curiosity and awakened my compassion. He seldom walked alone without muttering to himself, and he occasionally stormed about as if defying an army of invisible foes. Most of his leisure was spent in walking around, cursing and gesticulating as if possessed by a demon. He was evidently a wretched man, at war with his own soul and all the world around him. To be overheard by the children disturbed him very little. He made no more of our presence than that of the ducks and geese he met on the green. But when his gestures were most violent, ending with a threatening shake of the head and a sharp snap of his middle finger and thumb, I deemed it wise to keep at a safe distance from him.

One of the first circumstances that opened my eyes to the cruelties and wickedness of slavery and its hardening influences upon my old master, was his refusal to interpose his authority to protect and shield a young woman, a cousin of mine, who had been most cruelly abused and beaten by his overseer in Tuckahoe. This overseer, a Mr. Plummer, was, like most of his class, little less than a human brute; and, in addition to his general profligacy and repulsive coarseness, he was a miserable drunkard, a man not fit to have the management of a drove of mules. In one of his moments of drunken madness he committed the outrage which brought the young woman in question down to my old master's for protection. The poor girl, on her arrival at our house, presented a most pitiable appearance. She had left in haste and without preparation, and probably without the knowledge of Mr. Plummer. She had traveled twelve miles, barefooted, bare necked, and bare-headed. Her neck and shoulders were covered with scars, newly made; and, not content with marring her neck and shoulders with the cowhide, the cowardly wretch had dealt her a blow on the head with a hickory club, which cut a horrible gash, and left her face literally covered with blood. In this condition the poor young woman came down to implore protection at the hands of my old master. I expected to see him boil over with rage at the revolting deed, and to hear him fill the air with curses upon the brutal Plummer; but I was disappointed. He sternly told her in an angry tone, "She deserved every bit of it, and if she did not go home instantly he would himself take the remaining skin from her neck and back." Thus the poor girl was compelled to return without redress, and perhaps to receive an additional flogging for daring to appeal to authority higher than that of the overseer.

I did not at that time understand the philosophy of this treatment of my cousin. I think I now understand it. This treatment was a part of the system, rather than a part of the man. To have encouraged appeals of this kind would have occasioned much loss of time and would have left the overseer powerless to enforce obedience. Nevertheless, when a slave had nerve enough to go straight to his master with a well-founded complaint against an overseer, though he might be repelled and have even that of which he at the time complained repeated, and though he might be beaten by his master, as well as by the overseer, for his termerity, the policy of complaining was, in the end, generally vindicated by the relaxed rigor of the overseer's treatment. The latter became more careful and less disposed to use the lash upon such slaves thereafter.

The overseer very naturally disliked to have the ear of the master disturbed by complaints; and, either for this reason or because of advice privately given him by his employer, he generally modified the rigor of his rule after complaints of this kind had been made against him. For some cause or other, the slaves, no matter how often they were repulsed by their masters, were ever disposed to regard them with less abhorrence than the overseer. And yet these masters would often go beyond their overseers in wanton cruelty. They wielded the lash without any sense of responsibility. They could cripple or kill without fear of consequences. I have seen my old master when in a tempest of wrath, and full of pride, hatred, jealousy and revenge, seem a very fiend.

The circumstances which I am about to narrate and which gave rise to this fearful tempest of passion, were not singular, but very common in our slave-holding community.

The reader will have noticed that, among the names of slaves, that of Esther is mentioned. This was the name of a young woman who possessed that which was ever a curse to the slave girl—namely, personal beauty. She was tall, light-colored, well formed, and made a fine appearance. Esther was courted by " Ned Roberts," the son of a favorite slave of Col. Lloyd, and who was as fine-looking a young man as

Esther was a woman. Some slaveholders would have been glad to have promoted the marriage of two such persons, but for some reason Captain Anthony disapproved of their courtship. He strictly ordered her to quit the society of young Roberts, telling her that he would punish her severely if he ever found her again in his company. But it was impossible to keep this couple apart. Meet they would and meet they did. Had Mr. Anthony himself been a man of honor, his motives in this matter might have appeared more favorably. As it was, they appeared as abhorrent as they were contemptible. It was one of the damning characteristics of slavery that it robbed its victims of every earthly incentive to a holy life. The fear of God and the hope of heaven were sufficient to sustain many slave women amidst the snares and dangers of their strange lot; but they were ever at the mercy of the power, passion and caprice of their owners. Slavery provided no means for the honorable perpetuation of the race. Yet, despite of this destitution, there were many men and women among the slaves who were true and faithful to each other through life.

But to the case in hand. Abhorred and circumvented as he was, Captain Anthony, having the power, was determined on revenge. I happened to see its shocking execution, and shall never forget the scene. It was early in the morning, when all was still, and before any of the family in the house or kitchen had risen. I was, in fact, awakened by the heart-rending shrieks and piteous cries of poor Esther. My sleeping-place was on the dirt floor of a little rough closet which opened into the kitchen, and through the cracks in its unplaned boards I could distinctly see and hear what was going on, without being seen. Esther's wrists were firmly tied, and the twisted rope was fastened to a strong iron staple in a heavy wooden beam above, near the fire-place. Here she stood on a bench, her arms tightly drawn above her head. Her back and shoulders were perfectly bare. Behind her stood old master, cowhide in hand, pursuing his barbarous work with all manner of harsh, coarse, and tantalizing epithets. He was cruelly deliberate, and protracted the torture as one who was delighted with the agony of his victim. Again and again he drew the hateful scourge through his hand, adjusting it with a view of dealing the most pain-giving blow his strength and skill could inflict. Poor Esther had never before been severely whipped. Her shoulders were plump and tender. Each blow, vigorously laid on, brought screams from her as well as blood. "Have mercy! Oh, mercy!" she cried. "I won't do so no more." But her piercing cries seemed only to increase his fury. The whole scene, with all its attendant circumstances, was revolting and shocking to the last degree, and when the motives for the brutal castigation are known, language has no power to convey a just sense of its dreadful criminality. After laying on I dare not say how many stripes, old master untied his suffering victim. When let down she could scarcely stand. From my heart I pitied her, and child as I was, and new to such scenes, the shock was tremendous. I was terrified, hushed, stunned and bewildered. The scene here described was often repeated, for Edward and Esther continued to meet, notwithstanding all efforts to prevent their meeting.

Chapter VI.

A CHILD'S REASONING.

The author's early reflections on Slavery—Aunt Jennie and Uncle Noah—Presentment of one day becoming a freeman—Conflict between an overseer and a slave woman—Advantage of resistance— Death, of an overseer—Col. Lloyd's plantation home—Monthly distribution of food—Singing of Slaves—An explanation—The slaves' food and clothing—Naked children—Life in the quarter—Sleeping places—not beds—Deprivation of sleep—Care of nursing babies— Ash cake—Contrast.

THE incidents related in the foregoing chapter led me thus early to inquire into the origin and nature of slavery. Why am I a slave ? Why are some people slaves and others masters ? These were perplexing questions and very troublesome to my childhood. I was very early told by some one that " *God up in the shy* " had made all things, and had made black people to be slaves and white people to be masters. I was told too that God was good, and that He knew what was best for everybody. This was, however, less satisfactory than the first statement. It came point blank against all my notions of goodness. The case of Aunt Esther was in my mind. Besides, I could not tell how anybody could know that God made black people to be slaves. Then I found, too, that there were puzzling exceptions to this theory of slavery, in the fact that all black people were not slaves, and all white people were not masters.

An incident occurred about this time that made a deep impression on my mind. My Aunt Jennie and one of the men slaves of Captain Anthony ran away. A great noise was made about it. Old master was furious. He said he would follow them and catch them and bring them back, but he never did, and somebody told me that Uncle Noah and Aunt Jennie had gone to the free states and were free. Besides this occurrence, which brought much light to my mind on the subject, there were several slaves on Mr. Lloyd's place who remembered being brought from Africa. There were others who told me that their fathers and mothers were stolen from Africa.

This to me was important knowledge, but not such as to make me feel very easy in my slave condition. The success of Aunt Jennie and Uncle Noah in getting away from slavery was, I think, the first fact that made me seriously think of escape for myself. I could not have been more than seven or eight years old at the time of this occurrence, but young as I was I was already, in spirit and purpose, a fugitive from slavery.

Up to the time of the brutal treatment of my Aunt Esther, already narrated, and the shocking plight in which I had seen my cousin from Tuckahoe, my attention had not been especially directed to the grosser and more revolting features of slavery. I had, of course, heard of whippings and savage mutilations of slaves by brutal overseers, but happily for me I had always been out of the way of such occurrences. My play time was spent outside of the corn and tobacco fields, where the overseers and slaves were brought together and in conflict. But after the case of my Aunt Esther I saw others of the same disgusting and shocking nature. The one of these which agitated and distressed me most was the whipping of a woman, not belonging to my old master, but to Col. Lloyd. The charge against her was very common and very indefinite, namely, " *impudence.* " This crime could be committed by a slave in a hundred different ways, and depended much upon the temper and caprice of the overseer as to whether it was committed at all. He could create the offense whenever it pleased him. A look, a word, a gesture, accidental or intentional, never failed to be taken as impudence when he was in the right mood for such an offense. In this case there were all the necessary conditions for the commission of the crime charged. The offender was nearly white, to begin with ; she was the wife of a favorite hand on board of Mr. Lloyd's sloop, and was besides, the mother of five sprightly children. Vigorous and spirited woman that she was, a wife and a mother, with a predominating share of the blood of the master running in her veins, Nellie (for that was her name) had all the qualities essential to impudence to a slave overseer. My attention was called to the scene of the castigation by the loud screams and curses that proceeded from the direction of it. When I came near the parties engaged in the struggle the overseer had hold of Nellie, endeavoring with his whole strength to drag her to a tree against her resistance. Both his and her faces were bleeding, for the woman was doing her best. Three of her children were present, and though quite small, (from seven to ten years old, I should think), they gallantly took the side of their mother against the overseer, and pelted him well with stones and epithets. Amid the screams of the children, " *Let my mammy go ! Let my mammy go!*" the hoarse voice of the maddened overseer was heard in terrible oaths that he would teach her how to give a white man " *impudence*" The blood on his face and on hers attested her skill in the use of her nails, and his dogged determination to conquer. His purpose was to tie her up to a tree and give her, in slave-holding parlance, a " genteel flogging," and he evidently had not expected the stern and protracted resistance he was meeting, or the strength and skill needed to its execution. There were times when she seemed likely to get the better of the brute, but he finally overpowered her and succeeded in getting her arms firmly tied to the tree towards which he had been dragging her. The victim was now at the mercy of his merciless lash. What followed I need not here describe. The cries of the now helpless woman, while undergoing the terrible infliction, were mingled with the hoarse curses of the overseer and the wild cries of her distracted children. When the poor woman was untied her back was covered with blood. She was whipped, terribly whipped, but she was not subdued, and continued to denounce the overseer and to pour upon him every vile epithet of which she could think. Such floggings are seldom repeated on the same persons by overseers. They prefer to whip those who are the most easily whipped. The doctrine that submission to violence is the best cure for violence did not hold good as between slaves and overseers. He was whipped oftener who was whipped easiest. That slave who had the courage to stand up for himself against the overseer, although he might have many hard stripes at first, became while legally a slave virtually a freeman. " You can shoot me," said a slave to Rigby Hopkins, " but you can't whip me," and the result was he was neither whipped nor shot. I do not know that Mr. Sevier ever attempted to whip Nellie again. He probably never did, for he was taken sick not long after and died. It was commonly said that his death-bed was a wretched one, and that, the ruling passion being strong in death, he died flourishing the slave whip and with horrid oaths upon his lips. This death-bed scene may only be the imagining of the slaves. One thing is certain, that when he was in health his profanity was enough to chill the blood of an ordinary man. Nature, or habit, had given to his face an expression of uncommon savageness. Tobacco and rage had ground his teeth short, and nearly every sentence that he uttered was commenced or completed with an oath. Hated for his cruelty, despised for his cowardice, he went to his grave lamented by nobody on the place outside of his own house, if, indeed, he was even lamented there.

In Mr. James Hopkins, the succeeding overseer, we had a different and a better man; as good perhaps as any man could be in the position of a slave overseer. Though he sometimes wielded the lash, it was evident that he took no pleasure in it and did it with much reluctance. He stayed but a short time here, and his removal from the position was much regretted by the slaves generally. Of the successor of Mr. Hopkins shall have something to say at another time and in another place.

For the present we will attend to a further description of the business-like aspect of Col. Lloyd's *"Great House"* farm. There was always much bustle and noise here on the two days at the end of each month, for then the slaves belonging to the different branches of this great estate assembled here by their representatives, to obtain their monthly allowances of corn-meal and pork. These were gala days for the slaves of the outlying farms, and there was much rivalry among them as to who should be elected to go up to the Great House farm for the " *Allowances"* and indeed to attend to any other business at this great place, to them the capital of a little nation. Its beauty and grandeur, its immense wealth, its numerous population, and the fact that uncles Harry, Peter, and Jake, I the sailors on board the sloop, usually kept on sale trinkets which they bought in Baltimore to sell to their less fortunate fellow-servants, made a visit to the Great House farm a high privilege, and eagerly sought. It was valued, too, as a mark of distinction and confidence; but probably the chief motive among the competitors for the office was the opportunity it afforded to shake off the monotony of the field and to get beyond the overseer's eye and lash. Once on the road with an ox-team, and seated on the tongue of the cart, with no overseer to look after him, one felt comparatively free.

Slaves were expected to sing as well as to work. A silent slave was not liked, either by masters or overseers. *"Make a noise there ! Make a noise there ! "* and " bear a hand," were words usually addressed to slaves when they were silent. This, and the natural disposition of the negro to make a noise in the world, may account for the almost constant singing among them when at their work. There was generally more or less singing among the teamsters, at all times. It was a means of telling the overseer, in the distance, where they were and what they were about. But on the allowance days those commissioned to the Great House farm were peculiarly vocal. While on the way they would make the grand old woods for miles around reverberate with their wild and plaintive notes. They were indeed both merry and sad. Child as I was, these wild songs greatly depressed my spirits. Nowhere outside of dear old Ireland, in the days of want and famine, have I heard sounds so mournful.

In all these slave songs there was ever some expression of praise of the Great House farm—something that would please the pride of the Lloyds.

I am going away to the Great House farm,
O, yea! O, yea! O, yea! My old master is a good old master,
O, yea! O, yea! O, yea!

These words would be sung over and over again, with others, improvised as they went along—jargon, perhaps, to the reader, but full of meaning to the singers. I have sometimes thought that the mere hearing of these songs would have done more to impress the good people of the north with the soul-crushing character of slavery than whole volumes exposing the physical cruelties of the slave system; for the heart has no language like song. Many years ago, when recollecting my experience in this respect, I wrote of these slave songs in the following strain:

"I did not, when a slave, fully understand the deep meaning of those rude and apparently incoherent songs. I was, myself, within the circle, so that I could then neither hear nor see as those without might see and hear. They breathed the prayer and complaint of souls overflowing with the bitterest anguish. They depressed my spirits and filled my heart with ineffable sadness."

The remark in the olden time was not unfrequently made, that slaves were the most contented and happy laborers in the world, and their dancing and singing were referred to in proof of this alleged fact; but it was a great mistake to suppose them happy because they sometimes made those joyful noises. The songs of the slaves represented their sorrows, rather than their joys. Like tears, they were a relief to aching hearts. It is not inconsistent with the constitution of the human mind that it avails itself of one and the same method for expressing opposite emotions. Sorrow and desolation have their songs, as well as joy and peace.

It was the boast of slaveholders that their slaves enjoyed more of the physical comforts of life than the peasantry of any country in the world. My experience contradicts this. The men and the women slaves on Col. Lloyd's farm received as their monthly allowance of food, eight pounds of pickled pork, or its equivalent in fish. The pork was often tainted, and the fish were of the poorest quality. With their pork or fish, they had given them one bushel of Indian meal, unbolted, of which quite fifteen per cent, was more fit for pigs than for men. With this one pint of salt was given, and this was the entire monthly allowance of a full-grown slave, working constantly in the open field from morning till night every day in the month except Sunday. There is no kind of work which really requires a better supply of food to prevent physical exhaustion than the field work of a slave. The yearly allowance of clothing was not more ample than the supply of food. It consisted of two tow-linen shirts, one pair of trowsers of the same coarse material, for summer, and a woolen pair of trowsers and a woolen jacket for winter, with one pair of yarn stockings and a pair of shoes of the coarsest description. Children under ten years old had neither shoes, stockings, jackets, nor trowsers. They had two coarse tow-linen shirts per year, and when these were worn out they went naked till the next allowance day—and this was the condition of the little girls as well as of the boys. As to beds, they had none. One coarse blanket was given them, and this only to the men and women. The children stuck themselves in holes and corners about the quarters, often in the corners of huge chimneys, with their feet in the ashes to keep them warm. The want of beds, however, was not considered a great privation by the field hands. Time to sleep was of far greater importance. For when the day's work was done most of these had their washing, mending, and cooking to do, and having few or no facilities for doing such things, very many of their needed sleeping hours were consumed in necessary preparations for the labors of the coming day. The sleeping apartments, if they could have been properly called such, had little regard to comfort or decency. Old and young, male and female, married and single, dropped down upon the common clay floor, each covering up with his or her blanket, their only protection from cold or exposure. The night, however, was shortened at both ends. The slaves worked often as long as they could see, and were late in cooking and mending for the coming day, and at the first gray streak of the morning they were summoned to the field by the overseer's horn. They were whipped for over-sleeping more than for any other fault. Neither age nor sex found any favor. The overseer stood at the quarter door, armed with stick and whip, ready to deal heavy blows upon any who might be a little behind time. When the horn was blown there was a rush for the door, for the hindermost one was sure to get a blow from the overseer. Young mothers who worked in the field were allowed an hour about ten o'clock in the morning to go home to nurse their children. This was when they were not required to take them to the field-with them, and leave them upon " turning row," or in the corner of the fences.

As a general rule the slaves did not come to their quarters to take their meals, but took their ash-cake (called thus because baked in the ashes) and piece of pork, or their salt herrings, where they were at work.

But let us now leave the rough usage of the field, where vulgar coarseness and brutal cruelty flourished as rank as weeds in the tropics and where a vile wretch, in the shape of a man, rides, walks and struts about, with whip in hand, dealing heavy blows and leaving deep gashes on the flesh of men and women, and turn our attention to the less repulsive slave life as it existed in the home of my child- hood. Some idea of the splendor of that place sixty years ago has already been given. The contrast between the condition of the slaves and that of their masters was marvelously sharp and striking. There were pride, pomp and luxury on the one hand, servility, dejection, and misery on the other.

Chapter VII.

LUXURIES AT THE GREAT HOUSE.

Contrasts—Great House luxuries—Its hospitality—Entertainments— Fault-finding—Shameful humiliation of an old and faithful coachman—William Wilks—Curious incident—Expressed satisfaction not always genuine—Reasons for suppressing the truth.

T HE close-fisted stinginess that fed the poor slave on coarse corn-meal and tainted meat, that clothed him in crashy tow-linen and hurried him on to toil through the field in all weathers, with wind and rain beating through his tattered garments, and that scarcely gave even the young slave-mother time to nurse her infant in the fence-corner, wholly vanished on approaching the sacred precincts of the " Great House " itself. There the scriptural phrase descriptive of the wealthy found exact illustration. The highly-favored inmates of this mansion were literally arrayed in "purple and fine linen, and fared sumptuously *every* day." The table of this house groaned under the blood-bought luxuries gathered with pains-taking care at home and abroad. Fields, forests, rivers, and seas were made tributary. Immense wealth and its lavish expenditures filled the Great House with all that could please the eye or tempt the taste. Fish, flesh, and fowl were here in profusion. Chickens of all breeds; ducks of all kinds, wild and tame, the common and the huge Muscovite; Guinea fowls, turkeys, geese and pea-fowls; all were fat and fattening for the destined vortex. Here the graceful swan, the mongrel, the black-necked wild goose, partridges, quails, pheasants, pigeons and choice water fowl, with all their strange varieties, were caught in this huge net. Beef, veal, mutton, and venison, of the most select kinds and quality, rolled in bounteous profusion to this grand consumer. The teeming riches of the Chesapeake Bay, its rock perch, drums, crocus, trout, oysters, crabs, and terrapin were drawn hither to adorn the glittering table. The dairy, too, the finest then on the eastern shore of Maryland, supplied by cattle of the best English stock, imported for the express purpose, poured its rich donations of fragrant cheese, golden butter, and delicious cream to heighten the attractions of the gorgeous, unending round of feasting. Nor were the fruits of the earth overlooked. The fertile garden, many acres in size, constituting a separate establishment distinct from the common farm, with its scientific gardener direct from Scotland, a Mr. McDermott, and four men under his direction, was not behind, either in the abundance or in the delicacy of its contributions. The tender asparagus, the crispy celery, and the delicate cauliflower, egg plants, beets, lettuce, parsnips, peas, and French beans, early and late; radishes, cantelopes, melons of all kinds; and the fruits of all climes and of every description, from the hardy apples of the north to the lemon and orange of the south, culminated at this point. Here were gathered figs, raisins, almonds, and grapes from Spain, wines and brandies from France, teas of various flavor from China, and rich, aromatic coffee from Java, all conspiring to swell the tide of high life, where pride and indolence lounged in magnificence and satiety.

Behind the tall-backed and elaborately wrought chairs stood the servants, fifteen in number, carefully selected, not only with a view to their capacity and adeptness, but with especial regard to their personal appearance, their graceful agility, and pleasing address. Some of these servants, armed with fans, wafted reviving breezes to the over-heated brows of the alabaster ladies, whilst others watched with eager eye and fawn-like step, anticipating and supplying wants before they were sufficiently formed to be announced by word or sign.

These servants constituted a sort of black aristocracy. They resembled the field hands in nothing except then-color, and in this they held the advantage of a velvet-like glossiness, rich and beautiful. The hair, too, showed the same advantage. The delicately-formed colored maid rustled in the scarcely-worn silk of her young mistress, while the servant men were equally well attired from the overflowing wardrobe of their young masters, so that in dress, as well as in form and feature, in manner and speech, in tastes and habits, the distance between these favored few and the sorrow and hunger-smitten multitudes of the quarter and the field was immense.

In the stables and carriage-houses were to be found the same evidences of pride and luxurious extravagance. Here were three splendid coaches, soft within and lustrous without. Here, too, were gigs, phaetons, barouches, sulkeys, and sleighs. Here were saddles and harnesses, beautifully wrought and richly mounted. Not less than thirty-five horses of the best approved blood, both for speed and beauty, were kept only for pleasure. The care of these horses constituted the entire occupation of two men, one or the other of them being always in the stable to answer any call which might be made from the Great House. Over the way from the stable was a house built expressly for the hounds, a pack of twenty-five or thirty, the fare for which would have made glad the hearts of a dozen slaves. Horses and hounds, however, were not the only consumers of the slave's toil. The hospitality practiced at the Lloyd's would have astonished and charmed many a health-seeking divine or merchant from the north. Viewed from his table, and *not* from the field, Colonel Lloyd was, indeed, a model of generous hospitality. His house was literally a hotel for weeks, during the summer months. At these times, especially, the air was freighted with the rich fumes of baking, boiling, roasting, and broiling. It was something to me that I could share these odors with the winds, even if the meats themselves were under a more stringent monopoly. In master Daniel I had a friend at court, who would sometimes give me a cake, and who kept me well informed as to their guests and their entertainments. Viewed from Col. Lloyd's table who could have said that his slaves were not well clad and well cared for. Who would have said they did not glory in being the slaves of such a master ? Who but a fanatic could have seen any cause for sympathy for either master or slave ? Alas, this immense wealth, this gilded splendor, this profusion of luxury, this exemption from toil, this life of ease, this sea of plenty were not the pearly gates they seemed to a world of happiness and sweet content to be. The poor slave, on his hard pine plank, scantily covered with his thin blanket, slept more soundly than the feverish voluptuary who reclined upon his downy pillow. Food to the indolent is poison, not sustenance. Lurking beneath the rich and tempting viands were invisible spirits of evil, which filled the self-deluded gormandizer with aches and pains, passions uncontrollable, fierce tempers, dyspepsia, rheumatism, lumbago, and gout, and of these the Lloyds had a full share.

I had many opportunities of witnessing the restless dis-content and capricious irritation of the Lloyds. My fond-ness for horses attracted me to the stables much of the time.

The two men in charge of this establishment were old and young Barney—father and son. Old Barney was a fine-looking, portly old man of a brownish complexion, and a respectful and dignified bearing. He was much devoted to his profession, and held his office as an honorable one. He was a farrier as well as an ostler, and could bleed horses, remove lampers from their mouths and administer medicine to them. No one on the farm knew so well as old Barney what to do with a sick horse; but his office was not an enviable one, and his gifts and acquirements were of little advantage to him. In nothing was Col. Lloyd more unreasonable and exacting than in respect to the management of his horses. Any supposed inattention to these animals was sure to be visited with degrading punishment. His horses and dogs fared better than his men. Their beds were far softer and cleaner than those of his human cattle. No excuse could shield old Barney if the Colonel only suspected something wrong about his Horses, and consequently he was often punished when faultless. It was painful to hear the unreasonable and fretful scoldings administered by Col. Lloyd, his son Murray, and his sons-in-law, to this poor man. Three of the daughters of Col. Lloyd were married, and they with their husbands remained at the great house a portion of the year, and enjoyed the luxury of whipping the servants when they pleased. A horse was seldom brought out of the stable to which no objection could be raised. "There was dust in his hair ;" "there was a twist in his reins;" " his foretop was not combed; his mane did not lie straight;" "his head did not look well" his fetlocks had not been properly trimmed." Something was always wrong. However groundless the complaint, Barney must stand, hat in hand, lips sealed, never answering a word in explanation or excuse. In a free State, a master thus complaining without cause, might be told by his ostler : " Sir, I am sorry I cannot please you, but since I have done the best I can and fail to do so, your remedy is to dismiss me." But here the ostler must listen and tremblingly abide his master's behest. One of the most heart-saddening and humiliating scenes I ever witnessed was the whipping of old Barney by Col. Lloyd. These two men were both advanced in years; there were the silver locks of the master, and the bald and toil-worn brow of the slave—superior and inferior here, powerful and weak here, but *equals* before God. " Uncover your head," said the imperious master; he was obeyed. " Take off your jacket, you old rascal! " and off came Barney's jacket. " Down on your knees! " Down knelt the old man, his shoulders bare, his bald head glistening in the sunshine, and his aged knees on the cold, damp ground. In this humble and debasing attitude, that master, to whom he had devoted the best years and the best strength of his life, came forward and laid on thirty lashes with his horsewhip. The old man made no resistance, but bore it patiently, answering each blow with only a shrug of the shoulders and a groan. I do not think that the physical suffering from this infliction was severe, for the whip was a light riding-whip; but the spectacle of an aged man—a husband and a father—humbly kneeling before his fellow-man, shocked me at the time; and since I have grown older, few of the features of slavery have impressed me with a deeper sense of its injustice and barbarity than did this exciting scene. I owe it to the truth, however, to say that this was the first and last time I ever saw a slave compelled to kneel to receive a whipping.

Another incident, illustrating a phase of slavery to which I have referred in another connection, I may here mention. Besides two other coachmen, Col. Lloyd owned one named William Wilks, and his was one of the exceptionable cases where a slave possessed a surname, and was recognized by it, by both colored and white people. Wilks was a very fine-looking man. He was about as white as any one on the plantation, and in form and feature bore a very striking resemblance to Murray Lloyd. It was whispered and generally believed that William Wilks was a son of Col. Lloyd, by a highly favored slave woman, who was still on the plantation. There were many reasons for believing this whisper, not only from his personal appearance, but from the undeniable freedom which he enjoyed over all others, and his apparent consciousness of being something more than a slave to his master. It was notorious too that William had a deadly enemy in Murray Lloyd, whom he so much resembled, and that the latter greatly worried his father with importunities to sell William. Indeed, he gave his father no rest, until he did sell him to Austin Woldfolk, the great slave-trader at that time. Before selling him, however, he tried to make things smooth by giving William a whipping, but it proved a failure. It was a compromise, and like most such, defeated itself, —for Col. Lloyd soon after atoned to William for the abuse by giving him a gold watch and chain. Another fact somewhat curious was, that though sold to the remorseless Woldfolk, taken in irons to Baltimore, and cast into prison, with a view to being sent to the South, William outbid all his purchasers, paid for himself, and afterwards resided in Baltimore. How this was accomplished was a great mystery at the time, explained only on the supposition that the hand which had bestowed the gold watch and chain had also supplied the purchase-money, but I have since learned that this was not the true explanation. Wilks had many friends in Baltimore and Annapolis, and they united to save him from a fate which was one of all others most dreaded by the slaves. Practical amalgamation was however so common at the South, and so many circumstances pointed in that direction, that there was little reason to doubt that William Wilks was the son of Edward Lloyd. The real feelings and opinions of the slaves were not much known or respected by their masters. The distance between the two was too great to admit of such knowledge, and in this respect Col. Lloyd was no exception to the rule. His slaves were so numerous that be did not know them when he saw them. Nor, indeed, did all his slaves know him. It is reported of him, that, riding along the road one day, he met a colored man, and addressed him in what was the usual way of speaking to colored people on the public highways of the south: " Well, boy, who do you belong to ?" " To Col. Lloyd," replied the slave. "Well, does the Colonel treat you well?" "No, sir," was the ready reply. " What, does he work you hard ?" " Yes, sir." " Well, don't he give you enough to eat ? Yes, sir, he gives me enough to eat, such as it is." The Colonel rode on ; the slave also went on about his business, not dreaming that he had been conversing with his master. He thought and said nothing of the matter, until, two or three weeks afterwards, he was informed by his overseer that, for having found fault with his master, he was now to be sold to a Georgia trader. He was immediately chained and handcuffed ; and thus, without a moment's warning, he was snatched away, and forever sundered from his family and friends by a hand as unrelenting as that of death. This was the penalty of telling the simple truth, in answer to a series of plain questions. It was partly in consequence of such facts, that slaves, when inquired of as to their condition and the character of their masters, would almost invariably say that they were contented and their masters kind. Slaveholders are known to have sent spies among their slaves to ascertain, if possible, their views and feelings in regard to their condition; hence the maxim established among them, that " a still tongue makes a wise head." They would suppress the truth rather than take the consequences of telling it, and in so doing they prove themselves a part of the human family. I was frequently asked if I had a kind master, and I do not remember ever to have given a negative reply. I did not consider myself as uttering that which was strictly untrue, for I always measured the kindness of my master by the standard of kindness set up by the slaveholders around us.

Chapter VIII.

CHARACTERISTICS OF OVERSEERS.

Austin Gore—Sketch of his character—Overseers as a class—Their peculiar characteristics—The marked individuality of Austin-Gore —His sense of duty—Murder of poor Denby —Sensation—How Gore made his peace with Col. Lloyd—Other horrible murders—No laws for the protection of slaves possible of being enforced.

THE comparatively moderate rule of Mr. Hopkins as overseer on Col. Lloyd's plantation was succeeded by that of another, whose name was Austin Gore. I hardly know how to bring this man fitly before the reader; for Tinder him there was more suffering from violence and bloodshed than had, according to the older slaves, ever been experienced before at this place. He was an overseer, and possessed the peculiar characteristics of his class; yet to call him merely an overseer would not give one a fair conception of the man. I speak of overseers as a class, for they were such. They were as distinct from the slaveholding gentry of the South as are the fish-women of Paris and the coal-heavers of London distinct from other grades of society. They constituted, at the South, a separate fraternity. They were arranged and classified by that great law of attraction which determines the sphere and affinities of men and which ordains that men whose malign and brutal propensities preponderate over their moral and intellectual endowments shall naturally fall into the employments which promise the largest gratification to their predominating instincts or propensities. The office of overseer took this raw material of vulgarity and brutality and stamped it as a distinct class in southern life. But in this class, as in all other classes, there were sometimes persons of marked individuality, yet with a general resemblance to the mass. Mr. Gore was one of those to whom a general characterization would do no manner of justice. He was an overseer, but he was something more. With the malign and tyrannical qualities of an overseer he combined something of the lawful master. He had the artfulness and mean ambition of his class, without its disgusting swagger and noisy bravado. There was an easy air of independence about him, a calm self-possession, and at the same time a sternness of glance which well might daunt less timid hearts than those of poor slaves accustomed from childhood to cower before a driver's lash. He was one of those overseers who could torture the slightest word or look into impudence, and he had the nerve not only to resent, but to punish promptly and severely. There could be no answering back. Guilty or not guilty, to be accused was to be sure of a flogging. His very presence was fearful, and I shunned him as I would have shunned a rattlesnake. His piercing black eyes and sharp, shrill voice ever awakened sensations of dread. Other overseers, how brutal soever they might be, would sometimes seek to gain favor with the slaves by indulging in a little pleasantry; but Gore never said a funny thing or perpetrated a joke. He was always cold, distant, and unapproachable—the *overseer* on Col. Edward Lloyd's plantation—and needed no higher pleasure than the performance of the duties of his office. When he used the lash, it was from a sense of duty, without fear of consequences. There was a stern will, an iron-like reality about him, which would easily have made him chief of a band of pirates, had his environments been favorable to such a sphere. Among many other deeds of shocking cruelty committed by him was the murder of a young colored man named Bill Denby. He was a powerful fellow, full of animal spirits, and one of the most valuable of Col. Lloyd's slaves. In some way, I know not what, he offended this Mr. Austin Gore, and, in accordance with the usual custom, the latter undertook to flog him. He had given him but a few stripes when Denby broke away from him, plunged into the creek, and, standing there with the water up to his neck, refused to come out; whereupon, for this refusal, Gore *shot him dead!* It was said that Gore gave Denby three calls to come out, telling him that if he did not obey the last call he should shoot him. When the last call was given Denby still stood his ground, and Gore, without further parley or making any further effort to induce obedience, raised his gun deliberately to his face, took deadly aim at his standing victim, and with one click of the gun the mangled body sank out of sight, and only his warm red blood marked the place where he had stood.

This fiendish murder produced, as it could not help doing, a tremendous sensation. The slaves were panic-stricken, and howled with alarm. The atrocity roused my old master, and he spoke out in reprobation of it. Both he and Col. Lloyd arraigned Gore for his cruelty; but the latter, calm and collected as though nothing unusual had happened, declared that Denby had become unmanageable ; that he set a dangerous example to the other slaves, and that unless some such prompt measure was resorted to there would be an end of all rule and order on the plantation. That convenient covert for all manner of villainy and outrage; that cowardly alarm-cry that the slaves would "take the place," was pleaded, just as it had before been in thousands of similar cases. Gore's defense was evidently considered satisfactory, for he was continued in his office without being subjected to a judicial investigation. The murder was committed in the presence of slaves only, and they, being slaves, could neither institute a suit nor testify against the murderer. Mr. Gore lived in St. Michaels, Talbot Co., Maryland, and I have no reason to doubt, from what I know to have been the moral sentiment of the place, that he was as highly esteemed and as much respected as though his guilty soul had not been stained with innocent blood.

I speak advisedly when I say that in Talbot Co., Maryland, killing a slave, or any colored person, was not treated as a crime, either by the courts or the community. Mr. Thomas Lanman, ship carpenter of St. Michaels, killed two slaves, one of whom he butchered with a hatchet by knocking out his brains. He used to boast of having committed the awful and bloody deed. I have heard him do so laughingly, declaring himself a benefactor of his country and that "when others would do as much as he had done, they would be rid of the d—d niggers."

Another notorious fact which I may here state was the murder of a young girl between fifteen and sixteen years of age, by her mistress, Mrs. Giles Hicks, who lived but a short distance from Col. Lloyd's. This wicked woman, in the paroxysm of her wrath, not content with killing her victim, literally mangled her face and broke her breastbone. Wild and infuriated as she was, she took the precaution to cause the burial of the girl; but, the facts of the case getting abroad, the remains were disinterred and a coroner's jury assembled, who, after due deliberation, decided that " the girl had come to her death from severe beating." The offense for which this girl was thus hurried out of the world was this: she had been set that night, and several preceding nights, to mind

Mrs. Hicks' baby, and, having fallen into a sound sleep, the crying of the baby did not wake her, as it did its mother. The tardiness of the gild excited Mrs. Hicks, who, after calling her several times, seized a piece of fire-wood from the fire place and pounded in her skull and breast-bone till death ensued. I will not say that this murder most foul produced no sensation. It *did* produce a sensation. A warrant was issued for the arrest of Mrs. Hicks, but incredible to tell, for some reason or other, that warrant was never served, and she not only escaped consign punishment, but the pain and mortification as well, of being arraigned before a court of justice.

While I am detailing the bloody deeds that took place during my stay on Col. Lloyd's plantation, I will briefly narrate another dark transaction, which occurred about the time of the murder of Denby.

On the side of the river Wye opposite from Col. Lloyd's, there lived a Mr. Beal Bondley, a wealthy slaveholder. In the direction of his land, and near the shore, there was an excellent oyster fishing-ground, and to this sonic of Lloyd's slaves occasionally resorted in their little canoes, at night, with a view to make up the deficiency of their scanty allowance of food by the oysters that they could easily get there. Mr. Bondley took it into his head to regard this as a trespass, and while an old man slave was engaged in catching a few of the many millions of oysters that lined the bottom of the creek, to satisfy his hunger, the rascally Bondley, lying in ambush, without the slightest warning, discharged the contents of his musket into the back of the poor old man. As good fortune would have it, the shot did not prove fatal, and Mr. Bondley came over the next day to see Col. Lloyd about it. What happened between them I know not, but there was little said about it and nothing publicly done. One of the commonest sayings to which my ears early became accustomed, was, that it was " worth but a half a cent to kill a nigger, and half a cent to bury one." While I heard of numerous murders committed by slaveholders on the eastern shore of Maryland, I never knew a solitary instance where a slaveholder was either hung or imprisoned for having murdered a slave. The usual pretext for such crimes was that the slave had offered resistance. Should a slave, when assaulted, but raise his hand in self-defense, the white assaulting party was fully justified by southern law and southern public opinion in shooting the slave down, and for this there was no redress.

Chapter IX.

CHANGE OF LOCATION.

Miss Lucretia—Her kindness—How it was manifested—
"Ike"—A battle with him—Miss Lucretia's balsam—
Bread—How it was obtained—Gleams of sunlight amidst the
general darkness—Suffering from cold—How we took our
meal mush—Preparations for going to Baltimore—Delight
at the change—Cousin Tom's opinion of Baltimore—Arrival
there—Kind reception—Mr. and Mrs. Hugh Auld —Their
son Tommy—My relations to them—My duties—A turning
point in my life.

I have nothing cruel or shocking to relate of my own
personal experience while I remained on Col. Lloyd's
plantation, at the home of my old master. An occasional cuff
from Aunt Katy, and a regular whipping from old master,
such as any heedless and mischievous boy might get from
his father, is all that I have to say of this sort. I was not old
enough to work in the field, and there being little else than
field-work to perform, I had much leisure. The most I had
to do was to drive up the cows in the evening, to keep the
front yard clean, and to perform small errands for my young
mistress, Lucretia Auld. I had reasons for thinking this lady
was very kindly disposed towards me, and although I was not
often the object of her attention, I constantly regarded her as
my friend, and was always glad when it was my privilege to
do her a service. In a family where there was so much that was
harsh and indifferent, the slightest word or look of kindness
was of great value. Miss Lucretia—as we all continued to

call her long after her marriage—had bestowed on me such looks and words as taught me that she pitied me, if she did not love me. She sometimes gave me a piece of bread and butter, an article not set down in our bill of fare, but an extra ration aside from both Aunt Katy and old master, and given as I believed solely out of the tender regard she had for me. Then, too, I one day got into the wars with Uncle Abel's son " Ike," and got sadly worsted ; the little rascal struck me directly in the forehead with a sharp piece of cinder, fused with iron, from the old blacksmith's forgo, which made a cross in my forehead very plainly to be seen even now. The gash bled very freely, and I roared and betook myself home. The cold-hearted Aunt Katy paid no attention either to my wound or my roaring except to tell me it " served me right; I had no business with Ike ; it would do me good; I would now keep away from dem Lloyd niggers."Miss Lucrctia in this state of the case came forward, and called me into the parlor (an extra privilege of itself), and without using toward me any of the hard and reproachful epithets of Aunt Katy, quietly acted the good Samaritan. With her own soft hand she washed the blood from my head and face, brought her own bottle of balsam, and with the balsam wetted a nice piece of white linen and bound up my head. The balsam was not more healing to the wound in my head, than her kindness was healing to the wounds in my spirit, induced by the unfeeling words of Aunt Katy.

Miss Lucretia was after this yet more my friend I felt her to be such and I have no doubt that the simple act of binding up my head did much to awaken in her heart an interest in my welfare. It is quite true that this interest seldom showed itself in anything more than in giving me a piece of bread and butter, but this was a great favor on a slave plantation, and I was the only one of the children to whom such attention was paid. When very severely pinched with hunger, I had the habit of singing, which the good lady very soon came to understand, and when she heard me singing under her window I was very apt to be paid for my music.

Thus I had two friends, both at important points— Mas'r Daniel at the great house, and Miss Lucretia at home. From Mas'r Daniel I got protection from the bigger boys, and from Miss Lucretia I got bread by singing when I was hungry, and sympathy when I was abused by the termagant in the kitchen. For such friendship 1 was deeply grateful, and bitter as are my recollections of slavery, it is a true pleasure to recall any instances of kindness, any sunbeams of humane treatment, which found way to my soul, through the iron grating of my house of bondage. Such beams seem all the brighter from the general darkness into which they penetrate, and the impression they make there is vividly distinct.

As before intimated, I received no severe treatment from the hands of my master, but the insufficiency of both food and clothing was a serious trial to me, especially the lack of clothing. In hottest summer and coldest winter I was kept almost in a state of nudity. My only clothing—a little coarse sack-cloth or tow-linen sort of shirt, scarcely reaching to my knees, was worn night and day and changed once a week. In the day time I could protect myself by keeping on the sunny side of the house, or, in stormy weather, in the corner of the kitchen chimney. But the great difficulty was to keep warm during the night. The pigs in the pen had leaves, and the horses in the stable had straw, but the children had no beds. They lodged anywhere in the ample kitchen. I slept generally in a little closet, without even a blanket to cover me. In very cold weather I sometimes got down the bag in which corn was carried to the mill, and crawled into that. Sleeping there with my head in and my feet out, I was partly protected, though never comfortable. My feet have been so cracked with the frost that the pen with which I am writing might be laid in the gashes. Our corn meal mush, which was our only regular if not all-sufficing diet, was, when sufficiently cooled from the cooking, placed in a large tray or trough. This was set down either on the floor of the kitchen, or out of doors on the ground, and the children were called like so many pigs, and like so many pigs would come, some with oyster-shells, some with pieces of shingles, but none with spoons, and literally devour the mush. He who could eat fastest got most, and he who was strongest got the best place, but few left the trough really satisfied. I was the most unlucky of all, for Aunt Katy had no good feeling for me, and if I pushed the children, or if they told her anything unfavorable of me, she always believed the worst and was sure to whip me.

As I grew older and more thoughtful, I became more and more filled with a sense of my wretchedness. The unkindness of Aunt Katy, the hunger and cold I suffered, and the terrible reports of wrongs and outrages which came to my ear, together with what I almost daily witnessed, led me to wish 1 had never been born. I used to contrast my condition with that of the black-birds, in whose wild and sweet songs I fancied them so happy. Their apparent joy only deepened the shades of my sorrow. There are thoughtful days in the lives of children— at least there were in mine—when they grapple with the great primary subjects of knowledge, and reach in a moment conclusions which no subsequent experience can shake. I was just as well aware of the unjust, unnatural and murderous character of slavery, when nine years old, as I am now. Without any appeals to books, to laws, or to authorities of any kind, to regard God as "Our Father," condemned slavery as a crime.

I was in this unhappy state when I received from Miss Lucretia the joyful intelligence that my old master had determined to let me go to Baltimore to live with Mr. Hugh Auld, a brother to Mr. Thomas Auld, Miss Lucretia's husband. I shall never forget the ecstacy with which I received this information, three days before the time set for my departure. They were the three happiest days I had ever known. I spent the largest part of them in the creek, washing off the plantation scurf, and thus preparing for my now home. Miss Lucretia took a lively interest in getting me ready. She told me I must get all the dead skin off my feet and knees, for the people in Baltimore were very cleanly, and would laugh at me if I looked dirty; and besides she was intending to give me a pair of trowsers, but which I could not put on unless I got off all the dirt. This was a warning which I was bound to heed, for the thought of owning and wearing a pair of trowsers was great indeed. So I went at it in good earnest, working for the first time in my life in the hope of reward. I was greatly excited, and could hardly consent to sleep lest I should be left.

The ties that ordinarily bind children to their homes had no existence in my case, and in thinking of a home elsewhere, I was confident of finding none that I should relish less than the one I was leaving. If I should meet with hardship, hunger, and nakedness, I had known them all before, and I could endure them elsewhere, especially in Baltimore, for I had something of the feeling about that city that is expressed in the saying that " being hanged in England is better than dying a natural death in Ireland." I had the strongest desire to see Baltimore. My cousin Tom, a boy two or three years older than I, had been there, and, though not fluent in speech (he stuttered immoderately), he had inspired me with that desire by his eloquent descriptions of the place. Tom was

sometimes cabin-boy on board the sloop " Sally Lloyd "
(which Capt. Thomas Auld commanded), and when he came
home from Baltimore he was always a sort of hero amongst
us, at least till his trip to Baltimore was forgotten. I could
never tell him anything, or point out anything that struck me
as beautiful or powerful, but that he had seen something in
Baltimore far surpassing it. Even the " great house," with all
its pictures within and pillars without, he had the hardihood
to say, " was nothing to Baltimore." He bought a trumpet
(worth sixpence) and brought it home; told what he had seen
in the windows of the stores; that he had heard shooting-
crackers, and seen soldiers; that he had seen a steamboat,
and that they were ships in Baltimore that could carry four
such sloops as the " Sally Lloyd." He said a great deal about
the Market house ; of the ringing of the bells, and of many
other things which roused my curiosity very much, and indeed brightened my hopes of happiness in my new home.

"We sailed out of Miles River for Baltimore early on a
Saturday morning. I remember only the day of the week, for
at that time I had no knowledge of the days of the month,
nor indeed of the months of the year. On setting sail I walked
aft and gave to Col. Lloyd's plantation what I hoped would
be the last look I should give to it, or to any place like it.
After taking this last view, I quitted the quarter-deck, made
my way to the bow of the boat, and spent the remainder of
the day in looking ahead; interesting myself in what was in
the distance, rather than in what was near by, or behind. The
vessels sweeping along the bay were objects full of interest
to me. The broad bay opened like a shoreless ocean on my
boyish vision, filling me with wonder and admiration.

Late in the afternoon we reached Annapolis, but not
stopping there long enough to admit of going ashore. It was
the first large town I had ever seen, and though it was inferior

to many a factory village in New England, my feelings on seeing it were excited to a pitch very little below that reached by travelers at the first view of Rome. The donic of the State house was especially imposing, and surpassed in grandeur the appearance of the "great house" I had left behind. So the great world was opening upon me, and I was eagerly acquainting myself with its multifarious lessons.

We arrived in Baltimore on Sunday morning, and landed at Smith's wharf, not far from Bowly's wharf. We had on board a large flock of sheep for the Baltimore market; and after assisting in driving them to the slaughter house of Mr. Curtiss, on Loudon Slater's hill, I was conducted by Rich— one of the hands belonging to the sloop—to my new home on Alliciana street, near Gardiner's shipyard, on Fell's point. Mr. and Mrs. Hugh Auld, my new master and mistress, were both at home, and met me at the door, together with their rosy-cheeked little son Thomas, to take care of whom was to constitute my future occupation. In fact it was to "little Tommy," rather than to his parents, that old master made a present of me, and, though there was no *legal* form or arrangement entered into, I have no doubt that Mr. and Mrs. Auld felt that in due time I should be the legal property of their bright-eyed and beloved boy Tommy. I was especially struck with the appearance of my *new* mistress. Her face was lighted with the kindliest emotions ; and the reflex influence of her countenance, as well as the tenderness with which she seemed to regard me, while asking me sundry little questions, greatly delighted me, and lit up, to my fancy, the pathway of my future. Little Thomas was affectionately told by his mother, that " there was his Freddy," and that " Freddy would take care of him ;" and I was told to " be kind to little Tommy," an injunction I scarcely needed, for I had already fallen in love with the dear boy. With these little ceremonies

I was initiated into my new home, and entered upon my peculiar duties, then unconscious of a cloud to dim its broad horizon.

I may say here that I regard my removal from Col. Lloyd's plantation as one of the most interesting and fortunate events of my life. Viewing it in the light of human likelihoods, it is quite probable that but for the mere circumstance of being thus removed, before the rigors of slavery had fully fastened upon me; before my young spirit had been crushed under the iron control of the slave-driver; I might have continued in slavery until emancipated by the war.

Chapter X.

LEARNING TO READ.

City annoyances—Plantation regrets—My mistress—Her history— Her kindness—My master—His sourness—My comforts—Increased sensitiveness—My occupation— Learning to read—Baneful effects of slaveholding on my dear, good mistress—Mr. Hugh forbids Mrs. Sophia to teach me further—Clouds gather on my bright prospects —Master Auld's exposition of the Philosophy of Slavery— City slaves—Country slaves—Contrasts—Exceptions—Mr. Hamilton's two slaves—Mrs. Hamilton's cruel treatment of them—Piteous aspect presented by them—No power to come between the slave and slaveholder.

ESTABLISHED in my new home in Baltimore, I was not very long in perceiving that in picturing to myself what was to be my life there, my imagination had painted only the bright side; and that the reality had its dark shades as well as its light ones. The open country which had been so much to me was all shut out. Walled in on every side by towering brick buildings, the heat of the summer was intolerable to me, and the hard brick pavements almost blistered my feet. If I ventured out on to the streets, new and strange objects glared upon me at every step, and startling sounds greeted my cars from all directions. My country eyes and ears were confused and bewildered. Troops of hostile boys pounced upon me at every corner. They chased me, and called me " Eastern-Shore man," till really I almost wished myself back on the Eastern Shore. My new mistress happily proved to 'be all she had seemed, and in her presence I easily forgot all outside annoyances. Mrs. Sophia was naturally of an excellent disposition—kind, gentle, and cheerful. The supercilious contempt for the rights and feelings of others, and the petulance and bad humor which generally characterized slaveholding ladies, were all quite absent from her manner and bearing toward me.

She had never been a slaveholder—a thing then quite unusual at the South—but had depended almost entirely upon her own industry for a living. To this fact the dear lady no doubt owed the excellent preservation of her natural goodness of heart, for slavery could change a saint into a sinner, and an angel into a demon. I hardly knew how to behave towards "Miss Sopha," as I used to call Mrs. Hugh Auld. I could not approach her even as I had formerly approached Mrs. Thomas Auld. Why should I hang down my head, and speak with bated breath, when there was no pride to scorn me, no coldness to repel me, and no hatred to inspire me with fear ? I therefore soon came to regard her as something more akin to a mother than a slaveholding mistress. So far from deeming it impudent in a slave to look her straight in the face, she seemed ever to say, " look up, child; don't be afraid." The sailors belonging to the sloop esteemed it a great privilege to be the bearers of parcels or messages for her, for whenever they came, they wore sure of a most kind and pleasant reception. If little Thomas was her son, and her most dearly loved child, she made me something like his half-brother in her affections, if dear Tommy was exalted to a place on his mother's knee, " Freddy" was honored by a place at the mother's side. Nor did the slave-boy lack the caressing strokes of her gentle hand, soothing him into the consciousness that, though motherless, he was not friendless. Mrs. Auld was not only kind-hearted, but remarkably pious;

frequent in her attendance at public worship and much given to reading the Bible and to chanting hymns of praise when alone. Mr. Hugh was altogether a different character. He cared very little about religion ; knew more of the world and was more a part of the world, than his wife. He doubts less set out to be, as the world goes, a respectable man and to get on by becoming a successful ship-builder, in that city of ship-building. This was his ambition, and it fully occupied him. I was of course of very little consequence to him, and when he smiled upon me, as he sometimes did, the smile was borrowed from his lovely wife, and like borrowed light, was transient, and vanished with the source whence it was derived. Though I must in truth characterize Master Hugh as a sour man of forbidding appearance, it is due to him to acknowledge that he was never cruel to me, according to the notion of cruelty in Maryland. During the first year or two, he left me almost exclusively to the management of his wife. She was my law-giver. In hands so tender as hers, and in the absence of the cruelties of the plantation, I became both physically and mentally much more sensitive, and a frown from my mistress caused me far more suffering than had Aunt Katy's hardest cuffs. Instead of the cold, damp floor of my old master's kitchen, I was on carpets ; for the corn bag in winter, I had a good straw bed, well furnished with covers; for the coarse corn meal in the morning, I had good bread and mush occasionally ; for my old tow-linen shirt, I had good clean clothes. I was really well off. My employment was to run of errands, and to take care of Tommy; to prevent his getting in the way of carriages, and to keep him out of harm's way generally.

So for a time everything went well. I say for a time, because the fatal poison of irresponsible power, and the natural influence of slave customs, were not very long in making their impression on the gentle and loving disposition of my excellent mistress. She at first regarded me as a child, like any other. This was the natural and spontaneous thought; afterwards, when she came to consider me as property, our relations to each other were changed, but a nature so noble as hers could not instantly become perverted, and it took several years before the sweetness of her temper was wholly lost.

The frequent hearing of my mistress reading the Bible aloud, for she often read aloud when her husband was absent, awakened my curiosity in respect to this *mystery* of reading, and roused in me the desire to learn. Up to this time I had known nothing whatever of this wonderful art, and my ignorance and inexperience of what it-could do for me, as well as my confidence in my mistress, emboldened me to ask her to teach me to read. With an unconsciousness and inexperience equal to my own, she readily consented, and in an incredibly short time, by her kind assistance, I had mastered the alphabet and could spell words of three or four letters. My mistress seemed almost as proud of my progress as if I had been her own child, and supposing that her husband would be as well pleased, she made no secret of what she was doing for me. Indeed, she exultingly told him of the aptness of her pupil and of her intention to persevere, as she felt it her duty to do, in teaching me, at least, to read the Bible. And here arose the first dark cloud over my Baltimore prospects, the precursor of chilling blasts and drenching storms. Master Hugh was astounded beyond measure and, probably for the first time, proceeded to unfold to his wife the true philosophy of the slave system, and the peculiar rules necessary in the nature of the case to be observed in the management of human chattels. Of course he forbade her to give me any further instruction, telling her in the first place that to do so was unlawful, as it was also unsafe; "for," said he, "if you give a nigger an inch he will take an ell. Learning will spoil the best nigger in the world. If he learns to read the Bible it will forever unfit him to be a slave. He should know nothing but the will of his master, and learn to obey it. As to himself, learning will do him no good, but a great deal of harm, making him disconsolate and unhappy. If you teach him how to read, he'll want to know how to write, and this accomplished, he'll be running away with himself." Such was the tenor of Master Hugh's oracular exposition; and it must be confessed that he very clearly comprehended the nature and the requirements of the relation of master and slave. His discourse was the first decidedly anti-slavery lecture to which it had been my lot to listen. Mrs. Auld evidently felt the force of what he said, and,like an obedient wife, began to shape her course in the direction indicated by him. The effect of his words *on me* was neither slight nor transitory. His iron sentences, cold and harsh, sunk like heavy weights deep into my heart, and stirred up within me a rebellion not soon to be allayed.

This was a new and special revelation, dispelling a painful mystery against which my youthful understanding had struggled, and struggled in vain, to wit, the white man's power to perpetuate the enslavement of the black man. " Very well," thought I. " Knowledge unfits a child to be a slave." I instinctively assented to the proposition, and from that moment I understood the direct pathway from slavery to freedom. It was just what I needed, and it came to me at a time and from a source whence I least expected it. Of course I was greatly saddened at the thought of losing the assistance of my kind mistress, but the information so instantly derived, to some extent compensated me for the loss I had sustained in this direction. Wise as Mr. Auld was, he underrated my comprehension, and had little idea of the use to which I was capable of putting the impressive lesson he was giving to his wife. He wanted me to be a slave ; I had already voted against that on the home plantation of Col. Lloyd. That which he most loved I most hated ; and the very determination which he expressed to keep me in ignorance only rendered me the more resolute to seek intelligence. In learning to read, therefore, I am not sure that I do not owe quite as much to the opposition of my master as to the kindly assistance of my amiable mistress. I acknowledge the benefit rendered me by the one, and by the other, believing that but for my mistress I might have grown up in ignorance.

Chapter XI

GROWING IN KNOWLEDGE.

My mistress—Her slaveholding duties—Their effects on her originally noble nature—The conflict in her mind—She opposes my learning to read—Too late—She had given me the " inch," I was resolved to take the "ell"—How I pursued my study to read—My tutors—• What progress I made—Slavery—What I heard said about it—Thirteen years old—Columbian orator—Dialogue—Speeches—Sheridan —Pitt—Lords Chatham and Fox—Knowledge increasing—Liberty —Singing—Sadness—Unhappiness of Mrs. Sophia—My hatred of slavery—One Upas tree overshadows us all.

I lived in the family of Mr. Auld, at Baltimore, seven years, during which time, as the almanac makers say of the weather, my condition was variable. The most interesting feature of my history here was my learning, under somewhat marked disadvantages, to read and write. In attaining this knowledge I was compelled to resort to indirections by no means congenial to my nature, and which were really humiliating to my sense of condor and uprightness. My mistress, checked in her benevolent designs toward me, not only ceased instructing me herself, but set her face as a flint against my learning to read by any means. It is due to her to say, however, that she did not adopt this course in all its stringency at first. She either thought it unnecessary, or she lacked the depravity needed to make herself forget at once my human nature. She was, as I have said, naturally a kind and tender-hearted woman, and in the humanity of her heart and the simplicity of her mind, she set out, when I first went to live with her, to treat me as she supposed one human being ought to treat another.

Nature never intended that men and women should be either slaves or slaveholders, and nothing but rigid training long persisted in, can perfect the character of the one or the other.

Mrs. Auld was singularly deficient in the qualities of a slaveholder. It was no easy matter for her to think or to feel that the curly-headed boy, who stood by her side, and even leaned on her lap, who was loved by little Tommy, and who loved little Tommy in turn, sustained to her only the relation of a chattel. I was more than that; she felt me to be more than that. I could talk and sing; I could laugh and weep; I could reason and remember; I could love and hate. I was human, and she, dear lady, knew and felt me to be so. How could she then treat me as a brute, without a mighty struggle with all the noblest powers of her soul ? That struggle came, and the will and power of the husband were victorious. Her noble soul was overcome, and he who wrought the wrong was injured in the fall no less than the rest of the household. When I went into that household, it was the abode of happiness and contentment. The wife and mistress there was a model of affection and tenderness. Her fervent piety and watchful uprightness made it impossible to sec her without thinking and feeling that " that woman is a Christian." There was no sorrow nor suffering for which she had not a tear, and there was no innocent joy for which she had not a smile. She had bread for the hungry, clothes for the naked, and comfort for every mourner who came within her reach.

But slavery soon proved its ability to divest her of these excellent qualities, and her home of its early happiness.

Conscience cannot stand much violence. Once thoroughly injured, who is he who can repair the damage ? If it be broken toward the slave on Sunday, it will be toward the master on Monday. It cannot long endure such shocks. It must stand unharmed, or it does not stand at all. As my condition in the family waxed had, that of the family waxed no better. The first step in the wrong direction was the violence done to nature and to conscience in arresting the benevolence that would have enlightened my young mind. In ceasing to instruct me, my mistress had to seek to justify herself *to* herself, and once consenting to take sides in such a debate, she was compelled to hold her position. One needs little knowledge of moral philosophy to see where she inevitably landed. She finally became even more violent in her opposition to my learning to read than was Mr. Auld himself. Nothing now appeared to make her more angry than seeing me, seated in some nook or corner, quietly reading a book or newspaper. She would rush at me with the utmost fury, and snatch the book or paper from my hand, with something of the wrath and consternation which a traitor might be supposed to feel on being dis-covered in a plot by some dangerous spy. The conviction once thoroughly established in her mind, that education and slavery were incompatible with each other, I was most narrowly watched in all my movements. If I remained in a separate room from the family for any considerable length of time, I was sure to be suspected of having a book, and was at once called to give an account of myself. But this was too late: the first and nevcr-to-be-retraced step had been taken. Teaching me the alphabet had been the "inch" given, I was now waiting only for the opportunity to " take the ell."

Filled with the determination to learn to read at any cost, I hit upon many expedients to accomplish that much desired end. The plan which I mainly adopted, and the one which was the most successful, was that of using as teachers my young white playmates, with whom I met on the streets. I used almost constantly to carry a copy of Webster's spelling-book in my pocket, and when sent of errands, or when play-time was allowed me, I would step aside with my young friends and take a lesson in spelling. I am greatly indebted to these boys—Gustavus Dorgan. Joseph Bailey, Charles Farity, and William Cosdry.

Although slavery was a delicate subject and, in Mary-land, very cautiously talked about among grown up people, I frequently talked with the white boys about it, and that very freely. I would sometimes say to them, while seated on a curbstone or a cellar door, "I wish I could be free, as you will be when you get to be men." "You will be free, you know, as soon as you are twenty-one, and can go where you like, but I am a slave for life. Have I not as good a right to be free as you have ?" Words like these, I observed, always troubled them; and I had no small satisfaction in drawing out from them, as I occasionally did, that fresh and bitter condemnation of slavery which ever springs from natures unseared and unperverted. Of all consciences, let me have those to deal with, which have not been seared and bewildered with the cares and perplexities of life. I do not remember ever while I was in slavery, to have met with a *boy* who defended the system, but I do remember many times, when I was consoled by them, and by them encouraged to hope that something WOULD YET occur by Which I would he made free. Over and over again, they have told me that "they believed 1 had as good a right to be free *as they* had," and that " they did not believe God ever made any one to be a slave." It is easily seen that such little conversations with my playfellows had no tendency to weaken my love of liberty, nor to render me contented as a slave.

When I was about thirteen years old, and had succeeded in learning to read, every increase of knowledge, especially anything respecting the free states, was an additional weight to the almost intolerable burden of my thought—"*I am a slave for life.*" To my bondage I could see no end. It was a terrible reality, and I shall never be able to tell how sadly that thought chafed my young spirit. Fortunately or unfortunately, I had, by blacking boots for some gentlemen, earned a little money with which I purchased of Mr. Knight, on Thames street, what was then a very popular school book, viz., " The Columbian Orator," for which I paid fifty cents. I was led to buy this book by hearing some little boys say that they were going to learn some pieces out of it for the exhibition. This volume was indeed a rich treasure, and, for a time, every opportunity afforded me was spent in diligently perusing it. Among much other interesting matter, that which I read again and again with unflagging satisfaction was a short dialogue between a master and his slave. The slave is represented as having been recaptured in a second attempt to run away; and the master opens the dialogue with an upbraiding speech, charging the slave with ingratitude, and demanding to know what he has to say in his own defense. Thus upbraided and thus called upon to reply, the slave rejoins that he knows how little anything that he can say will avail, seeing that he is completely in the hands of his owner; and with noble resolution, calmly says, " I submit to my fate." Touched by the slave's answer, the master insists upon his further speaking, and recapitulates the many acts of kindness which he has performed toward the slave, and tells him he is permitted to speak for himself. Thus invited, the quondam slave made a spirited defense of himself, and thereafter the whole argument for and against slavery is brought out. The master was vanquished at every turn in the argument, and, appreciating the fact, he generously and meekly emancipates the slave, with his best wishes for his prosperity.

It is unnecessary to say that a dialogue with such an origin and such an end, read by me when every nerve of my being was in revolt at my own condition as a slave, affected me most powerfully. I could not help feeling that the day might yet come when the well-directed answers made by the slave to the master, in this instance, would find a counterpart in my own experience. This, however, was not all the fanaticism which I found in the Columbian Orator. I met there one of Sheridan's mighty speeches on the subject of Catholic Emancipation, Lord Chatham's speech on the American War, and speeches by the great William Pitt, and by Fox. These were all choice documents to me, and I read them over and over again, with an interest ever increasing, because it was ever gaining in intelligence; for the more I read them the better I understood them. The reading of these speeches added much to my limited stock of language, and enabled me to give tongue to many interesting thoughts which had often flashed through my mind and died away for want of words in which to give them utterance. The mighty power and heart-searching directness of truth penetrating the heart of a slave-holder and compelling him to yield up his earthly interests to the claims of eternal justice, were finely illustrated in the dialogue, and from the speeches of Sheridan I got a bold and powerful denunciation of oppression and a most brilliant vindication of the rights of man.

Here was indeed a noble acquisition. If I had ever wavered under the consideration that the Almighty, in some way, had ordained slavery and willed my enslavement for His own glory, I wavered no longer. I had now penetrated to the secret of all slavery and of all oppression, and had ascertained their true foundation to be in the pride, the power and the avarice of man. With a book in my hand so redolent of the principles of liberty, and with a perception of my own human nature and of the facts of my past and present experience, I was equal to a contest with the religious advocates of slavery, whether white or black ; for blindness in this matter was not confined to the white people. I have met, at the south, many good, religious colored people who were under the delusion that God required them to submit to slavery and to wear their chains with meekness and humility. I could entertain no such nonsense as this, and I quite lost my patience when I found a colored man weak enough to believe such stuff. Nevertheless, eager as I was to partake of the tree of knowledge, its fruits were bitter as well as sweet. " Slaveholders," thought I, " are only a band of successful robbers, who, leaving their own homes, went into Africa for the purpose of stealing and reducing my people to slavery." I loathed them as the meanest and the most wicked of men. And as I read, behold! the very discontent so graphically predicted by Master Hugh had already come upon me. I was no longer the light-hearted, glee-some boy full of mirth and play, that I was when I landed in Baltimore. Light had penetrated the moral dungeon where I had lain, and I saw the bloody whip for my back and the iron chain for my feet, and my *good, kind* master was the author of my situation. The revelation haunted me, stung me, and made me gloomy and miserable. As I writhed under the sting and torment of this knowledge I almost envied my fellow slaves their stupid indifference. It opened my eyes to the horrible pit, and revealed the teeth of the frightful dragon that was ready to pounce upon me ; but alas, it opened no way for my escape. 1 wished myself a beast, a bird, anything rather than a slave. I was wretched and gloomy beyond my ability to describe. This everlasting thinking distressed and tormented me; and yet there was no getting rid of this subject of my thoughts. Liberty, as the inestimable birthright of every man, converted every object into an asserter of this right. I heard it in every sound, and saw it in every object. It was ever present to torment me with a sense of my wretchedness. The more beautiful and charming were the smiles of nature, the more horrible and desolate was my condition. I saw nothing without seeing it, and I heard nothing without hearing it. I do not exaggerate when I say that it looked at me in every star, smiled in every calm, breathed in every wind and moved in every storm. I have no doubt that my state of mind had something to do with the change in treatment which my mistress adopted towards me. I can easily believe that my leaden, downcast, and disconsolate look was very offensive to her. Poor lady! She did not understand my trouble, and I could not tell her. Could I have made her acquainted with the real state of my mind and given her the reasons therefor, it might have been well for both of us. As it was, her abuse fell upon me like the blows of the false prophet upon his ass; she did not know that an angel stood in the way. Nature made us friends, but slavery had made us enemies. My interests were in a direction opposite to hers, and we both had our private thoughts and plans. She aimed to keep me ignorant, and I resolved to *know,* although knowledge only increased my misery. My feelings were not the result of any marked cruelty in the treatment I received; they sprung from the consideration of my being a slave at all. It was *slavery,* not its mere *incidents* that I hated. I had been cheated. I saw through the attempt to keep me in ignorance. I saw that slaveholders would have gladly made me believe that, in making a slave of me and in making slaves of others, they were merely acting under the authority of God, and I felt to them as to robbers and deceivers. The feeding and clothing me well could not atone for taking my liberty from me. The smiles of my mistress could not remove the deep sorrow that dwelt in my young bosom.   Indeed, these came, in time, but to deepen my sorrow.   She had changed, and the reader will see that I too, had changed.   We were both victims to the same overshadowing evil, *she* as mistress, I as slave. I will not censure her harshly.

Chapter XII.

RELIGIOUS NATURE AWAKENED.

Abolitionists spoken of—Eagerness to know the meaning of word-Consults the dictionary — Incendiary information—The enigma solved— "Nat Turner" insurrection—Cholera—Religion—Methodist minister—Religious impressions—Father Lawson —His character and occupation'—His influence over me—Our mutual attachment—New hopes and aspirations—Heavenly light—Two Irishmen on wharf—Conversation with them—Learning to write—My aims.

I N the unhappy state of mind described in the foregoing chapter, regretting my very existence because doomed to a life of bondage, and so goaded and wretched as to be even tempted at times to take my own life, I was most keenly sensitive to know any and everything possible that had any relation to the subject of slavery. I was all ears, all eyes, whenever the words slave or slavery dropped from the lips of any white person, and more and more frequently occasions occurred when these words became leading ones in high, social debate at our house. Very often I would overhear Master Hugh, or some of his company, speak with much warmth of the " *abolitionists.*" *Who* or what the *abolitionists* were, I was totally ignorant. I found, however, that whoever or whatever they might be, they were most cordially hated and abused by slaveholders of every grade. I very soon discovered too, that slavery was, in some sort, under consideration whenever the abolitionists were alluded to. This made the term a very interesting one to me. If a slave had made good his escape from slavery, it was generally alleged that he had been persuaded and assisted to do so by the abolitionists. If a slave killed his master, or struck down his overseer, or set fire to his master's dwelling, or committed any violence or crime, out of the common way, it was certain to be said that such a crime was the legitimate fruits of the abolition movement.' Hearing such charges often repeated, 1, naturally enough, received the impression that abolition—whatever else it might be — was not unfriendly to the slave, nor very friendly to the slaveholder. I therefore set about finding out, if possible, *who* and *what* the abolitionists were, and *why* they were so obnoxious to the slaveholders. The dictionary offered me very little help. It taught me that abolition was "the act of abolishing;" but it left me in ignorance at the very point where I most wanted information, and that was, as to the thing to be abolished. A city newspaper—the "Baltimore *American"*—gave me the incendiary information denied me by the dictionary. In its columns I found that on a certain day a vast number of petitions and memorials had been presented to Congress, praying for the abolition of slavery in the District of Columbia, and for the abolition of the slave trade between the States of the Union. This was enough. The vindictive bitterness, the marked caution, the studied reserve, and the ambiguity practiced by our white folks when alluding to this subject, was now fully explained. Ever after that, when I heard the word abolition, I felt the matter one of a personal concern, and I drew near to listen whenever I could do so, without seeming too solicitous and prying. There was HOPE in those words. Ever and anon too, I could see some terrible denunciation of slavery in our papers,—copied from abolition papers at the North,—and the injustice of such denunciation commented on. These I read with avidity. I had a deep satisfaction in the thought that the rascality of slave-holders was not concealed from the eyes of the world, and that I was not alone in abhorring the cruelty and brutality of slavery. A still deeper train of thought was stirred. I saw that there was fear as well as rage in the manner of speaking of the abolitionists, and from this I inferred that they must have some power in the country, and I felt that they might perhaps succeed in their designs. When I met with a slave to whom I deemed it safe to talk on the subject, I would impart to him so much of the mystery as I had been able to penetrate. Thus the light of this grand movement broke in upon my mind by degrees ; and I must say that ignorant as I was of the philosophy of that movement, I believed in it from the first, and I believed in it, partly, because I saw that it alarmed the consciences of the slaveholders. The insurrection of Nat Turner had been quelled, but the alarm and terror which it occasioned had not subsided. The cholera was then on its way to this country, and I remember thinking that God was angry with the white people because of their slaveholding wickedness, and therefore his judgments were abroad in the land. Of course it was impossible for me not to hope much for the abolition movement when I saw it supported by the Almighty, and armed with DEATH.

Previously to my contemplation of the anti-slavery move-ment and its probable results, my mind had been seriously awakened to the subject of religion. I was not more than thirteen years old, when,in my loneliness and destitution,I longed for some one to whom 1 could go, as to a father and protector. The preaching of a white Methodist minister, named Hanson, was the means of causing me to feel that in God I had such a friend. He thought that all men, great and small, bond and free, were sinners in the sight of God :

that they were by nature rebels against his government; and that they must repent of their sins, and be reconciled to God through Christ. I cannot say that I had a very distinct notion of what was required of me, but one thing I did know well: that I was wretched and had no means of making myself otherwise. I consulted a good colored man named Charles Lawson, and in tones of holy affection he told me to pray, and to " cast all my care upon God." This I sought to do ; and though for weeks I was a poor, broken-hearted mourner, traveling through doubts and fears, I finally found my burden lightened, and my heart relieved. I loved all mankind, slaveholders not excepted, though I abhorred slavery more than ever. I saw the world in a new light, and my great concern was to have everybody converted. My desire to learn increased, and especially did I want a thorough acquaintance with the contents of the Bible. I have gathered scattered pages of the Bible from the filthy street-gutters, and washed and dried them, that in moments of leisure I might get a word or two of wisdom from them. While thus religiously seeking knowledge, I became acquainted with a good old colored man named Law-son. This man not only prayed three times a day, but he prayed as he walked through the streets, at his work, on his dray — everywhere. His life was a life of prayer, and his words when he spoke to any one, were about a better world. Uncle Lawson lived near Master Hugh's house, and becoming deeply attached to him, I went often with him to prayer-meeting and spent much of my leisure time on Sunday with him. The old man could read a little, and I was a great help to him in making out the hard words, for I was a better reader than he. I could teach him " the letter," but he could teach me " the spirit," and refreshing times we had together, in singing and praying. These meetings went on for a long time without the knowledge either of Master Hugh or my mistress. Both knew, however, that I had become religious, and seemed to respect my conscientious piety. My mistress was still a professor of religion, and belonged to class. Her leader was no less a person than Rev. Beverly Waugh, the presiding elder, and afterwards one of the bishops of the Methodist Episcopal church.

In view of the cares and anxieties incident to the life she was leading, and especially in view of the separation from religious associations to which she was subjected, my mistress had, as I have before stated, become lukewarm, and needed to be looked up by her leader. This often brought Mr. Waugh to our house, and gave me an opportunity to hear him exhort and pray. But my chief instructor in religious matters was Uncle Lawson. He was my spiritual father and I loved him intensely, and was at his house every chance I could get. This pleasure, however, was not long unquestioned. Master Hugh became averse to our intimacy, and threatened to whip me if I ever went there again. I now felt myself persecuted by a wicked man, and I W*ould* go. The good old man had told me that the " Lord had great work for me to do," and I must prepare to do it; that he had been shown that I must preach the gospel. His words made a very deep impression upon me, and I verily felt that some such work was before me, though 1 could not see how I could ever engage in its performance. " The good Lord would bring it to pass in his own good time," he said, and that I must go on reading and studying the Scriptures. This advice and these suggestions were not without their influence on my character and destiny. He fanned my already intense love of knowledge into a flame by assuring me that I was'to be a useful man in the world. When I would say to him, "How can these things be? and what can I do?" his simple reply was, " *Trust in the Lord.*" When I would tell him, " I am a slave, and a slave for life, how can I do anything ?" he would quietly answer, "The *Lord* can make you free, my dear; all things arc possible with Him; only have *faith* in God. ' Ask, and it shall be given you.' If you want liberty, ask the Lord lor it *in* FAITH, *and He will give it to you.*""

Thus assured and thus cheered on under the inspiration of hope, I worked and prayed with a light heart, believing that my life was under the guidance of a wisdom higher than my own. With all other blessings sought at the mercy seat, I always prayed that God would, of His great mercy, and in His own good time, deliver me from my bondage.

I went, one day, on the wharf of Mr. Waters, and seeing two Irishmen unloading a scow of stone or ballast, I went on board unasked, and helped them. When we had finished the work one of the men came to me, aside, and asked me a number of questions, and among them if I were a slave ? I told him " I was a slave for life." The good Irishman gave a shrug,and seemed deeply affected, He said it was a pity so fine a little fellow as I should be a slave for life. They both had much to say about the matter, and expressed the deepest sympathy with me, and the most decided hatred of slavery. They went so far as to tell me that I ought to run away and go to the north ; that I should find friends there, and that I should then be as free as anybody. I pretended not to be interested in what they said, for I feared they might he treacherous. White men were not unfrequently known to encourage slaves to escape, and then, to get the reward, they would kidnap them and return them to their masters. While I mainly inclined to the notion that these men were honest and meant me no ill, I feared it might be otherwise. I nevertheless remembered their words and their advice, and looked forward to an escape to the north as a possible means of gaining the liberty for which my heart panted. It was not my enslavement at the then present time which most affected me; the being a slave *for life* was the saddest thought. I was too young to think of running away immediately ; besides, I wished to learn to write before going, as I might have occasion to write my own pass. I now not only had the hope of freedom, but a foreshadowing of the means by which I might some day gain that inestimable boon. Meanwhile I resolved to add to my educational attainments the art of writing.

After this manner I began to learn to write. I was much in the ship-yard—Master Hugh's, and that of Durgan & Bailey, and I observed that the carpenters, after hewing and getting ready a piece of timber to use, wrote on it the initials of the name of that part of the ship for which it was intended. When, for instance, a piece of timber was ready for the starboard side, it was marked with a capital " S." A piece for the larboard side was marked " L."; larboard forward was marked "L. F.;" larboard aft was marked " L. A." ; starboard aft, " S. A." ; and starboard forward, " S. F." I soon learned these letters, and for what they were placed on the timbers.

My work now was to keep fire under the steam-box, and to watch the ship-yard while the carpenters had gone to dinner. This interval gave me a fine opportunity for copying the letters named. 1 soon astonished myself with the ease with which I made the letters, and the thought was soon present, "If I can make four letters 1 can make more." Having made these readily and easily, when I met boys about the Bethel church or on any of our play-grounds, I entered the lists with them in the art of writing, and would make the letters which I had been so fortunate as to learn, and ask them to " beat that if they could." With play-mates for my teachers, fences and pavements for my copy-books, and chalk for my pen and ink, I learned to write. I however adopted, afterward, various methods for improving my hand.

The most successful was copying the *italics* in Webster's spelling-book until I could make them all without looking on the book. By this time my little " Master Tommy" had grown to be a big boy, and had written over a number of copy-books and brought them home.' They had been shown to the neighbors, had elicited due praise, and had been laid carefully away. Spending parts of my time both at the ship-yard and the house, I was often the lone keeper of the latter as of the former. When my mistress left me in charge of the house 1 had a grand time. I got Master Tommy's copy-books and a pen and ink, and in the ample spaces between the lines I wrote other lines as nearly like his as possible. The process was a tedious one, and I ran the risk of getting a flogging for marking the highly-prized copy-books of the oldest son. In addition to these opportunities, sleeping as I did in the kitchen loft, a room seldom visited by any of the family, I contrived to get a flour-barrel up there and a chair, and upon the head of that barrel I have written, or endeavored to write, copying from the Bible and the Methodist hymn-book, and other books which I had accumulated, till late at night, and when all the family were in bed and asleep. I was supported in my endeavors by renewed advice and by holy promises from the good father Lawson, with whom I continued to meet and pray and read the Scriptures. Although Master Hugh was aware of these meetings, I must say for his credit that he never executed his threats to whip me for having thus innocently employed my leisure time.

Chapter XIII.

THE VICISSITUDES OF SLAVE LIFE.

Death of old Master's son Richard speedily followed by that of old Master—Valuation and division of all the property, including the slaves—Sent for to come to Hillsborough to be valued and divided — Sad prospects and grief — Parting — Slaves have no voice in deciding their own destinies— General dread of falling into Master Andrew's hands— His drunkenness—Good fortune in falling to Miss Lucretia— She allows my return to Baltimore—Joy at Master Hugh's— Heath of Miss Lucretia—Master Thomas Auld's second marriage — The new wife unlike the old — Again removed from Master Hugh's—Reasons for regret—Plan of escape.

I must now ask the reader to go back with me a little in point of time, in my humble story, and notice another circumstance that entered into my slavery experience, and which, doubtless, has had a share in deepening my horror of slavery and of my hostility toward those men and measures that practically uphold the slave system.

It has already been observed that though I was, after my removal from Col. Lloyd's plantation, in *form* the slave of Master Hugh Auld, I was *in fact* and in *law* the slave of my old master, Capt. Anthony. Very well. In a very short time after I went to Baltimore my old master's youngest son, Richard, died; and in three years and six months after, my old master himself died, leaving, to share the estate, only his daughter Lucretia and his son Andrew. The old man died while on a visit to his daughter in Hillsborough, where Capt. Auld and Mrs. Lucretia now lived. Master Thomas, having given up the command of Col. Lloyd's sloop, was now keeping store in that town.

Cut off thus unexpectedly, Capt. Anthony died intestate, and his property must be equally divided between his two children, Andrew and Lucretia.

The valuation and division of slaves among contending heirs was a most important incident in slave life. The characters and tendencies of the heirs were generally well understood by the slaves who were to be divided, of whom all had their aversions and their preferences. But neither their aversions nor their preferences availed anything.

On the death of old master I was immediately sent for to be valued and divided with the other property. Personally, my concern was mainly about my possible removal from the home of Master Hugh, for up to this time there had no dark clouds arisen to darken the sky of that happy abode. It was a sad day to me when I left for the Eastern Shore, to be valued and divided, as it was for my dear mistress and teacher, and for little Tommy. We all three wept bitterly, for we were parting, and it might be we were parting forever. No one could tell amongst which pile of chattels I might be flung. Thus early, I got a foretaste of that painful uncertainty which in one form or another was ever obtruding itself in the pathway of the slave. It furnished me a new insight into the unnatural power to which I was subjected. Sickness, adversity, and death may interfere with the plans and purposes of all, but the slave had the added danger of changing homes, in the separations unknown to other men. Then, too, there was the intensified degradation of the spectacle. What an assemblage ! Men and women, young and old, married and single; moral and thinking human beings, in open contempt of their humanity, leveled at a blow with horses, sheep, horned cattle, and swine. Horses and men, cattle and women, pigs and children all holding the same rank in the scale of social existence, and all subjected to the same narrow inspection, to ascertain their value in gold and silver — the only standard of worth applied by slaveholders to their slaves. Personality swallowed up in the sordid idea of property! Manhood lost in chattelhood!

The valuation over, then came the division and apportionment. Our destiny was to be *fixed for life,* and we had no more voice in the decision of the question than the oxen and cows that stood chewing at the hay-mow. One word of the appraisers, against all preferences and prayers, could sunder all the ties of friendship and affection, even to separating husbands and wives, parents and children. We were all appalled before that power which, to human seeming, could, in a moment, bless or blast us. Added to this dread of separation, most painful to the majority of the slaves, we all had a decided horror of falling into the hands of Master Andrew, who was distinguished for his cruelty and intemperance.

Slaves had a great dread, very naturally, of falling into the hands of drunken owners. Master Andrew was a confirmed sot, and had already by his profligate dissipation wasted a large portion of his father's property. To fall into his hands, therefore, was considered as the first step toward being sold away to the far South. He would no doubt spend his fortune in a few years, it was thought, and his farms and slaves would be sold at public auction, and the slaves hurried away to the cotton-fields and rice-swamps of the burning South. This was cause of deep consternation.

The people of the North, and free people generally, I think, have less attachment to the places where they are born and brought up than had the slaves. Their freedom to come and go, to be here or there, as they list, prevents any extravagant attachment to any one particular place.

On the other hand, the slave was a fixture; he had no choice, no goal, but was pegged down to one single spot, and must take root there or nowhere. The idea of removal elsewhere came generally in shape of a threat, and in punishment for crime. It was therefore attended with fear and dread. The enthusiasm which animates the bosoms of young freemen, when they contemplate a life in the far West, or in some distant country, where they expect to rise to wealth and distinction, could have no place in the thought of the slave; nor could those from whom they separated know anything of that cheerfulness with which friends and relations yield each other up, when they feel that it is for the good of the departing one that he is removed from his native place. Then, too, there is correspondence and the hope of reunion, but with the slaves, all these mitigating circumstances were wanting. There was no improvement in condition *probable* — no correspondence *possible* — no reunion attainable. His going out into the world was like a living man going into the tomb, who, with open eyes, sees himself buried out of sight and hearing of wife, children, and friends of kindred tie.

In contemplating the likelihoods and possibilities of our circumstances, I probably suffered more than most of my fellow-servants. I had known what it was to experience kind and even tender treatment; they had known nothing of the sort. Life to them had been rough and thorny, as well as dark. They had—most of them— lived on my old master's farm in Tuckahoe, and had felt the rigors of Mr. Plummer's rule. He had written his character on the living parchment of most of their backs, and left them seamed and callous; my' back (thanks to my early removal to Baltimore) was yet tender. I had left a kind mistress in tears when we parted, and the probability of ever seeing her again, trembling in the balance, as it were, could not fail to excite in me alarm and agony. The thought of becoming the slave of Andrew Anthony—who but a few days before the division, had, in my presence, seized my brother Perry by the throat, dashed him on the ground, and with the heel of his boot stamped him on the head, until the blood gushed from his nose and ears—was terrible! This fiendish proceeding had no better apology than the fact that Perry had gone to play when Master Andrew wanted him for some trifling service. After inflicting this cruel treatment on my brother, observing me, as I looked at him in astonishment, he said, " *That's* the way I'll serve you, one of these days"; meaning, probably, when I should come into his possession. This threat, the reader' may well suppose, was not very tranquilizing to my feelings.

At last the anxiety and suspense were ended; and ended, thanks to a kind Providence, in accordance with my wishes. I fell to the portion of Mrs. Lucretia, the dear lady who bound up my head in her father's kitchen, and shielded me from the maledictions of Aunt Katy.

Capt. Thomas Auld and Mrs. Lucretia at once decided on my return to Baltimore. They knew how warmly Mrs. Hugh Auld was attached to me, and how delighted Tommy would be to see me, and withal, having no immediate use for me, they willingly concluded this arrangement.

I need not stop to narrate my joy on finding myself back in Baltimore. I was just one month absent, but the time seemed fully six months.

I had returned to Baltimore but a short time when the tidings reached me that my kind friend, Mrs, Lucretia, was dead. She left one child, a daughter, named Amanda, of whom I shall speak again. Shortly after the death of Mrs.

Lucretia, Master Andrew died, leaving a wife and one child. Thus the whole family of Anthonys, as it existed -when I went to Col. Lloyd's place, was swept away during the first five years' time of my residence at Master Hugh Auld's in Baltimore.

No especial alteration took place in the condition of the slaves, in consequence of these deaths, yet I could not help the feeling that I was less secure now that Mrs. Lucretia was gone. While she lived, I felt that I had a strong friend to plead for me in any emergency.

In a little book which I published six years after my escape from slavery, entitled, " Narrative of Frederick Douglass,"— when the distance between the past then described and the present was not so great as it is now— speaking of these changes in my master's family, and their results, I used this language: " Now all the property of my old master, slaves included, was in the hands of strangers — strangers who had had nothing to do in its accumulation. Not a slave was left free. All remained slaves, from the youngest to the oldest. If any one thing more than another in my experience has served to deepen my conviction of the infernal character of slavery and fill me with unutterable loathing of slaveholders, it is their base ingratitude to my poor old grandmother. She had served my old master faithfully from youth to old age. She had been the source of all his wealth ; she had peopled his plantation with slaves; she had become a great-grandmother in his service. She had rocked him in his infancy, attended him in his childhood, served him through life, and at his death wiped from his icy brow the cold death-sweat, and closed his eyes forever. She was nevertheless a slave — a slave for life — a slave in the hands of strangers; and in their hands she saw her children, her grandchildren, and her great-grandchildren, divided like so many sheep ; and this without being gratified with the small privilege of a single word as to their or her own destiny. And to cap the climax of their base ingratitude, my grandmother, who was now very old, having outlived my old master and all his children, having seen the beginning and end of them, her present owner—his grandson — finding that she was of but little value ; that her frame was already racked with the pains of old age and that complete helplessness was fast stealing over her once active limbs— took her to the woods, built her a little hut with a mud chimney and then gave her the *bounteous* privilege of there supporting herself in utter loneliness ; thus virtually turning her out to die. If my poor, dear old grandmother now lives, she lives to remember and mourn over the loss of children, the loss of grandchildren and the loss of great-grandchildren. They are, in the language of Whittier, the slave's poet:

'Gone, gone, sold and gone,
To the rice-swamp dank and lone;
Where the slave-whip ceaseless swings.
Where the noisome insect stings,
Where the fever-demon strews
Poison with the falling dews,
Where the sickry sunbeams glare
Through the hot and misty air:-

Gone, gone, sold and gone,
To the rice-swamp, dank and lone,
From Virginia's hills and waters— '
Woe is me, my stolen daughters!'

" The hearth is desolate. The unconscious children who once sang and danced in her presence are gone. She gropes her way, in the darkness of age, for a drink of water. Instead of the voices of her children, she hears by day the moans of the clove, and by night the screams of the hideous owl. All is gloom. The grave is at the door; and now, weighed down by the pains and aches of old age, when the head inclines to the feet, when the beginning and ending of human existence meet, and helpless infancy, and painful old age combine together, at this time,—this most needed time for the exercise of that tenderness and affection which children only can bestow on a declining parent, — my poor old grandmother, the devoted mother of twelve children, is left all alone, in yonder little hut, before a few dim cinders."

Two years after the death of Mrs. Lucretia, Master Thomas married his second wife. Her name was Rowena Hamilton, the eldest daughter of Mr. William Hamilton, a rich slaveholder on the Eastern Shore of Maryland, who lived about five miles from St. Michaels, the then place of Master Thomas Auld's residence.

Not long after his marriage, Master Thomas had a misunderstanding with Master Hugh, and, as a means of punishing him, ordered him to send me home. As the ground of the misunderstanding will serve to illustrate the character of Southern chivalry and Southern humanity, fifty years ago, I will relate it.

Among the children of my Aunt Milly was a daughter named Henny. When quite a child, Henny had fallen into the fire and had burnt her hands so badly that they were of very little use to her. Her fingers were drawn almost into the palms of her hands. She could make out to do something, but she was considered hardly worth the having — of little more value than a horse with a broken leg. This unprofitable piece of property, ill-shapen, and disfigured, Capt. Auld sent off to Baltimore.

After giving poor Henny a fair trial, Master Hugh and his wife came to the conclusion that they had no use for the poor cripple, and they sent her back to Master Thomas. This the latter took as an act of ingratitude on the part of his brother and, as a mark of his displeasure, required him to send me immediately to St. Michaels, saying, " if he cannot keep Hen, he shan't have Fred."

Here was another shock to my nerves, another breaking up of my plans, and another severance of my religious and social alliances. I was now a big boy. I had become quite useful to several young colored men, who had made me their teacher. I had taught some of them to read, and was accustomed to spend many of my leisure hours with them. Our attachment was strong, and I greatly dreaded the separation. But, with slaves, regrets are unavailing ; my wishes were nothing ; my happiness was the sport of my master.

My regrets at leaving Baltimore now were not for the same reasons as when I before left the city to be valued and handed over to a new owner.

A change had taken place, both in Master Hugh and in his once pious and affectionate wife. The influence of brandy and bad company on him, and of slavery and social isolation on her, had wrought disastrously upon the characters of both. Thomas was no longer " little Tom-my," but was a big boy and had learned to assume towards me the airs of his class. My condition, therefore, in the house of Master Hugh was not by any means so comfortable as in former years. My attachments were now outside of our family. They were to those to whom I imparted instruction, and to those little white boys from whom I received instruction. There, too, was my dear old father, the pious Lawson, who was in all the Christian graces the very counterpart of " Uncle Tom" — the resemblance so perfect that he might have been the original of Mrs. Stowe's Christian hero. The thought of leaving these dear friends greatly troubled me, for I was going without the hope of ever returning again ; the feud being most bitter, and apparently wholly irreconcilable.

In addition to the pain of parting from friends, as I supposed, forever, I had the added grief of neglected chances of escape to brood over. I had put off running away until I was now to be placed where opportunities for escape would be much more difficult, and less frequent.

As we sailed down the Chesapeake bay, on board the sloop Amanda, to St Michaels, and were passed by the steamers plying between Baltimore and Philadelphia, I formed many a plan for my future, beginning- and ending in the same determination — to find some way yet of escape from slavery.

Chapter XIV.

EXPERIENCE IN
ST. MICHAELS.

St. Michaels and its inhabitants—Capt. Auld—His new wife—Sufferings from hunger—Forced to steal—Argument in vindication thereof—Southern camp-meeting—What Capt. Auld did there— Hopes—Suspicions—The result— Faith and works at variance— Position in the church —Poor Cousin Henny—Methodist Preachers Their disregard of the slaves—One exception —Sabbath-school— How and by whom broken up—Sad change in my prospects— Covey, the negro-breaker.

S T. Michaels, the village in which was now my new home, compared favorably with villages in slave States generally, at this time—1833. There were a few comfortable dwellings in it, but the place as a whole wore a dull, slovenly, enterprise-forsaken aspect. The mass of the buildings were of wood; they had never enjoyed the artificial adornment of paint, and time and storms had worn off the bright color of the wood, leaving them almost as black as buildings charred by a conflagration.

St. Michaels had, in former years, enjoyed some reputation as a ship-building community, but that business had almost entirely given place to oyster-fishing for the Baltimore and Philadelphia markets, a course of life highly unfavorable to morals, industry, and manners. Miles river was broad, and its oyster-fishing grounds were extensive, and the fishermen were, during autumn, winter and spring, often out all day and a part of the night. This exposure was an excuse for carrying with them, in considerable quantities, spirituous liquors, the then supposed best antidote for cold. Each canoe was supplied with its jug of rum, and tippling among this class of the citizens became general. This drinking habit, in an ignorant population, fostered coarseness, vulgarity, and an indolent disregard for the social improvement of the place, so that it was admitted by the few sober thinking people who remained there, that St. Michaels was an unsaintly, as well as unsightly place.

I went to St. Michaels to live in March, 1833. I know the year, because it was the one succeeding the first cholera in Baltimore, and was also the year of that strange phenomenon when the heavens seemed about to part with their starry train. I witnessed this gorgeous spectacle, and was awe-struck. The air seemed filled with bright descending messengers from the sky. It was about daybreak when I saw this sublime scene. I was not without the suggestion, at the moment, that it might be the harbinger of the coming of the Son of Man; and in my then state of mind I was prepared to hail Him as my friend and deliverer. I had read that the " stars shall fall from heaven," and they were now falling. I was suffering very much in my mind. It did seem that every time the young tendrils of my affection became attached they were rudely broken by some unnatural outside power; and 1 was looking away to heaven for the rest denied me on earth.

But to my story. It was now more than seven years since I had lived with Master Thomas Auld, in the family of my old master, Capt. Anthony, on the home plantation of Col. Lloyd. I knew him then as the husband of old master's daughter; I had now to know him as my master. All my lessons concerning his temper and disposition, and the best methods of pleasing him, were yet to be learned. Slaveholders, however, were not very ceremonious in approaching a slave, and my ignorance of the new material in the shape of a master was but transient. Nor was my new mistress long in making known her animus. Unlike Miss Lucretia, whom I remembered with the tenderness which departed blessings leave, Mrs. Rowena Auld was as cold and cruel as her husband was stingy, and possessed the power to make him as cruel as herself, while she could easily descend to the level of his meanness.

As long as I lived in Mr. Hugh Auld's family, in whatever changes came over them there had always been a bountiful supply of food. Now, for the first time in seven years, 1 realized the pitiless pinchings of hunger. So wretchedly starved were we that we were compelled to live at the expense of our neighbors, or to steal from the home larder. This was a hard thing to do; but after much reflection I reasoned myself into the conviction that there was no other way to do, and that after all there was no wrong in it. Considering that my labor and person were the property of Master Thomas, and that I was deprived of the necessaries of life—neeessaries obtained by my own labor—it was easy to deduce the right to supply myself with what was my own. It was simply appropriating what was my own to the use of my master, since the health and strength derived from such food were exerted in his service. To be sure, this was stealing, according to the law and gospel I heard from the pulpit; but I had begun to attach less importance to what dropped from that quarter on such points. It was not always convenient to steal from Master, and the same reason why I might innocently steal from him did not seem to justify me in stealing from others. In the case of my Master it was a question of removal—the taking his meat out of one tub and putting it in another; the ownership of the meat was not affected by the transaction. At first he owned it in the tub, and last he owned it in me. His meat-house was not always open. There was a strict watch kept in that point, and the key was carried in Mrs. Auld's pocket. We were oftentimes severely pinched with hunger, when meat and bread were mouldering under lock and key. This was so, when she knew we were nearly half starved; and yet with saintly air she would each morning kneel with her husband and pray that a merciful God would " bless them in basket and store, and save them at last in His kingdom." But I proceed with my argument.

It was necessary that the right to steal from others should be established; and this could only rest upon a wider range of generalization than that which supposed the right to steal from my master. It was some time before I arrived at this clear right. To give some idea of my train of reasoning, I will state the case as I laid it out in my mind. " I am," I thought, " not only the slave of Master Thomas, but I am the slave of society at large. Society at large has bound itself, in form and in fact, to assist Master Thomas in robbing me of my rightful liberty, and of the just reward of my labor; therefore, whatever rights I have against Master Thomas I have equally against those confederated with him in robbing me of liberty. As society has marked me out as privileged plunder, on the principle of self-preservation, I am justified in plundering in turn. Since each slave belongs to all, all must therefore belong to each." I reasoned further, that within the bounds of his just earnings the slave was fully justified in helping himself to the gold and silver, and the best apparel of his master, or that of any other slave-holder; and that such taking was not stealing, in any just sense of the word.

The morality of free society could have no application to slave society. Slaveholders made it almost impossible for the slave to commit any crime, known either to the laws of God or to the laws of man. If he stole, he but took his own; if he killed his master, he only imitated the heroes of the revolution. Slaveholders I held to be individually and collectively responsible for all the evils which grew out of the horrid relation, and I believed they would be so held in the sight of God. To make a man a slave was to rob him of moral responsibility. Freedom of choice is the essence of all accountability. But my kind readers are probably less concerned about what were my opinions than about that which more nearly touched my personal experience, albeit my opinions have, in some sort, been the outgrowth of my experience.

When I lived with Capt. Auld I thought him incapable of a noble action. His leading characteristic was intense selfishness. I think he was himself fully aware of this fact, and often tried to conceal it. Capt. Auld was not born a slaveholder. He was not a birthright member of the slave-holding oligarchy. He was only a slaveholder by marriage-right ; and of all slaveholders these were by far the most exacting. There was in him all the love of domination, the pride of mastery, and the swagger of authority; but his rule lacked the vital element of consistency. He could be cruel; but his methods of showing it were cowardly, and evinced his meanness, rather than his spirit. His commands were strong, his enforcements weak.

Slaves were not insensible to the whole-souled qualities of a generous, dashing slaveholder, who was fearless of consequences, and they preferred a master of this bold and daring kind, even with the risk of being shot down for impudence, to the fretful little soul who never used the lash but at the suggestion of a love of gain.

Slaves too, readily distinguish between the birthright bearing of the original slaveholder, and the assumed attitudes of the accidental slaveholder; and while they could have no respect for either, they despised the latter more than the former.

The luxury of having slaves to wait upon him was new to Master Thomas, and for it he was wholly unprepared. He was a slaveholder, without the ability to hold or manage his slaves. Failing to command their respect, both himself and wife were ever on the alert lest some indignity should be offered them by the slaves.

It was in the month of August, 1833, when I had become almost desperate under the treatment of Master Thomas, and entertained more strongly than ever the oft-repeated determination to run away, that a circumstance occurred which seemed to promise brighter and better days for us all. At a Methodist camp-meeting, held in the Bay side (a famous place for camp-meetings), about eight miles from St. Michaels, Master Thomas came out with a profession of religion. He had long been an object of interest to the church, and to the ministers, as I had seen by the repeated visits and lengthy exhortations of the latter. He was a fish quite worth catching, for he had money and standing. In the community of St. Michaels he was equal to the best citizen. He was strictly temperate, and there was little to do for him in order to give him the appearance of piety and to make him a pillar of the church. Well, the camp-meeting continued a week ; people gathered from all parts of the country, and two steamboats came loaded from Baltimore. The ground was happily chosen ; seats were arranged, a stand erected and a rude altar fronting the preacher's stand, fenced in, with straw in it, making a soft kneeling place for the accommodation of mourners. This place would have held at least one hundred persons. In front and on the sides of the preacher's stand, and outside the long rows of seats, rose the first class of stately tents, each vieing with the other in strength, neatness, and capacity for accommodation. Behind this first circle of tents was another,less imposing, which reached around the camp-ground to the speaker's stand. Outside this second class of tents were covered wagons, ox-carts, and vehicles of every shape and size. These served as tents for their owners. Outside of these, huge fires were burning in all directions, where roasting and boiling and frying were going on, for the benefit of those who were attending to their spiritual welfare within the circle. *Behind* the preacher's stand, a narrow space was marked out for the use of the colored people. There were no seats provided for this class of persons, and if the preachers addressed them at all, it was in an *aside.* After the preaching was over, at every service, an invitation was given to mourners to come forward into the pen; and in some cases, ministers wont out to persuade men and women to come in. By one of these ministers Master Thomas was persuaded to go inside the pen. I was deeply interested in that matter, and followed ; and though colored people were not allowed either in the pen, or in front of the preacher's stand, I ventured to take my stand at a sort of half-way place between the blacks and whites, where I could distinctly see the movements of the mourners, and especially the progress of Master Thomas. " If he has got religion," thought I, " he will emancipate his slaves; or, if he should not do so much as this, he will at any rate behave towards us more kindly, and feed us more generously than he has heretofore done." Appealing to my own religious experience, and judging my master by what was true in my own case, I could not regard him as soundly converted, unless some such good results followed his profession of religion. But in my expectations I was doubly disappointed: Master Thomas was *Master Thomas* still. The fruits of his righteousness were to show themselves in no such way as I had anticipated. His conversion was not to change his relation toward men—at any rate not toward BLACK men—but toward God. My faith, I confess, was not great. There was something in his appearance that in my mind cast a doubt over his conversion. Standing where I did, I could see his every movement. I watched very narrowly while he remained in the pen; and although I saw that his face was extremely red, and his hair disheveled, and though I heard him groan, and saw a stray tear halting on his cheek, as if inquiring, " which way shall I go ?"—I could not wholly confide in the genuineness of the conversion. The hesitating behavior of that tear-drop, and its loneliness, distressed me, and cast a doubt upon the whole transaction, of which it was a part. But people said, " Capt. Auld has come through," and it was for me to hope for the best. I was bound in charity to do this, for I, too, was religious, and had been in the church full three years, although now I was not more than sixteen years old. Slaveholders may sometimes have confidence in the piety of some of their slaves, but slaves seldom have confidence in the piety of their masters. " He can't go to heaven without blood on his skirts," was a settled point in the creed of every slave one which rose superior to all teachings to the contrary and stood forever as a fixed fact. The highest evidence of his acceptance with God which the slaveholder could give the slave, was the emancipation of his slaves. This was proof to us that he was willing to give up all to God, and for the sake of God, and not to do this was, in our estimation, an evidence of hard-heartedness, and was wholly inconsistent with the idea of genuine conversion. I had read somewhere, in the Methodist Discipline, the following question and answer: "Question. What shall be done for the extirpation of slavery?" "Answer. We declare that we are as much as ever convinced of the great evil of slavery; therefore, no slaveholder shall be eligible to any official station in our church." These words sounded in my ears for a long time, and encouraged me to hope. But, as I have before said, I was doomed to disappointment. Master Thomas seemed to be aware of my hopes and expectations concerning him. I have thought before now that he looked at me in answer to my glances, as much as to say, " I will teach you, young man, that though I have parted with my sins, I have not parted with my sense. I shall hold my slaves, and go to heaven too."

There was always a scarcity of good-nature about the man; but now his whole countenance was *soured* all over with the *seemings* of piety, and he became more rigid and. stringent in his exactions. If religion had any effect at all on him, it made him more cruel and hateful in all his ways. Do I judge him harshly ? God forbid. Capt. Auld made the greatest professions of piety. His house was literally a house of prayer. In the morning and in the evening loud prayers and hymns were heard there, in which both himself and wife joined; yet no more nor better meal was distributed at the quarters, no more attention was paid to the moral welfare of the kitchen, and nothing was done to make us feel that the heart of Master Thomas was one whit better than it was before he went into the little pen, opposite the preacher's stand on the camp-ground. Our hopes, too, founded on the discipline, soon vanished; for he was taken into the church at once, and before he was out of his term of probation he led in class. He quite distinguished himself among the brethren as a fervent exhorter. His progress was almost as rapid as the growth of the fabled vine of Jack and the Bcan-Stalk. No man was more active in revivals, or would go more miles to assist in carrying them on, and in getting outsiders interested in religion. His house, being one of the holiest in St. Michaels,

became the " preachers' home." They evidently liked to
share his hospitality; for while he *starved* us, he stuffed them
three or four of these "ambassadors" not unfrequently being
there at a time and all living on the fat of the land while
we in the kitchen' were worse than hungry. Not often did
we get a smile of recognition from these holy men. They
seemed about as unconcerned about our getting to heaven
as about our getting out of slavery. To this general charge I
must make one exception— the Reverend George Cookman.
Unlike Rev. Messrs. Storks, Ewry, Nicky, Humphrey, and
Cooper (all of whom were on the St. Michaels circuit),
he kindly took an interest in our temporal and spiritual
welfare. Our souls and our bodies were alike sacred in his
sight, and he really had a good deal of genuine anti-slavery
feeling mingled with his colonization ideas. There was not
a slave in our neighborhood who did not love and venerate
Mr. Cookman. It was pretty generally believed that he had
been instrumental in bringing one of the largest slaveholders in that neighborhood — Mr. Samuel Harrison —to
emancipate all his slaves, and the general impression about
Mr. Cookman was, that whenever he met slaveholders he
labored faithfully with them, as a religious duty, to induce
them to liberate their bondmen. When this good man was at
our house, we were all sure to be called in to prayers in the
morning; and he was not slow in making inquiries as to the
state of our minds, nor in giving us a word of exhortation
and of encouragement. Great was the sorrow of all the slaves
when this faithful preacher of the gospel was removed from
the circuit. He was an eloquent preacher, and possessed what
few ministers, south of Mason and Dixon's line, possessed
or dared to show ; viz., a warm and philanthropic heart. This
Mr. Cookman was an Englishman by birth, and perished on

board the ill-fated steamship " President," while on his way to England.

But to my experience with Master Thomas after his conversion. In Baltimore I could occasionally get into a Sabbath-school amongst the free children and receive lessons with the rest; but having already learned to read and write I was more a teacher than a scholar, even there. When, however, I went back to the eastern shore and was at the house of Master Thomas, I was not allowed either to teach or to be taught. The whole community among the whites, with but one single exception, frowned upon everything like imparting instruction, either to slaves or to free colored persons. That single exception, a pious young man named Wilson, asked me one day if I would like to assist him in teaching a little Sabbath-school at the house of a free colored man named James Mitchell. The idea to me was a delightful one and I told him that I would gladly devote to that most laudable work as many of my Sabbaths as I could command. Mr. Wilson soon mustered up a dozen old spelling-books and a fewTestaments,and we commenced operations with some twenty pupils in our school. Here, thought I, is something worth living for. Here is a chance for usefulness. The first Sunday passed delightfully, and I spent the week after very joyously. I could not go to Baltimore, where was the little company of young friends who had been so much to me there, and from whom I felt parted forever, but I could make a little Baltimore here. At our second meeting I learned there were some objections to the existence of our school; and, surely enough, we had scarcely got to work —*good* work, simply teaching a few colored children how to read the gospel of the Son of God — when in rushed a mob, headed by two class-leaders, Mr. Wright Fairbanks and Mr. Garrison West, and with them Master Thomas. They were armed with sticks and other missiles and drove us off, commanding us never again to meet for such a purpose. One of this pious crew told me that as for me, I wanted to be another Nat Turner, and that, if I did not look out, I should get as many balls in me as Nat did into him. Thus ended the Sabbath-school; and the reader will not be surprised that this conduct, on the part of class-leaders and professedly holy men, did not serve to strengthen my religious convictions. The cloud over my St. Michaels home grew heavier and blacker than ever.

It was not merely the agency of Master Thomas in breaking up our Sabbath-school, that shook my confidence in the power of that kind of southern religion to make men wiser or better, but I saw in him all the cruelty and meanness *after* his conversion which he had exhibited before that time. His cruelty and meanness were especially displayed in his treatment of my unfortunate cousin Henny, whose lameness made her a burden to him. I have seen him tie up this lame and maimed woman and whip her in a manner most brutal and shocking ; and then with blood-chilling blasphemy he would quote the passage of scripture, " That servant which knew his lord's will and prepared not himself, neither did according to his will, shall be beaten with many stripes." He would keep this lacerated woman tied up by her wrists to a bolt in the joist, three, four, and five hours at a time. He would tie her up early in the morning, whip her with a cowskin before breakfast, leave her tied up, go to his store, and, returning to dinner,repeat the casti-gation, laying the rugged lash on flesh already raw by repeated blows. He seemed desirous to get the poor girl out of existence, or at any rate off his hands. In proof of this, he afterwards gave her away to his sister Sarah (Mrs. Cline), but as in the case of Mr. Hugh, Henny was soon returned on his hands. Finally, upon a pretense that he could do nothing for her

(I use his own words), he " set her adrift to take care of herself." Here was a recently converted man, holding with tight grasp the well-framed and able-bodied slaves left him by old master — the persons who in freedom could have taken care of themselves; yet turning loose the only cripple among them, virtually to starve and die.

No doubt, had Master Thomas been asked by some pious northern brother, why he held slaves ? his reply would have been precisely that which many another slaveholder has returned to the same inquiry, viz.: "I hold my slaves for their own good."

The many differences springing up between Master Thomas and myself, owing to the clear perception I had of his character, and the boldness with which I defended myself against his capricious complaints, led him to declare that I was unsuited to his wants; that my city life had affected me perniciously; that in fact it had almost ruined me for every good purpose, and had fitted me for everything bad. One of my greatest faults, or offences, was that of letting his horse get away and go down to the farm which belonged to his father-in-law. The animal had a liking for that farm with which I fully sympathized. Whenever I let it out it would go dashing down the road to Mr. Hamilton's, as if going on a grand frolic. My horse gone, of course I must go after it. The explanation of our mutual attachment to the place is the same — the horse found good pasturage, and I found there plenty of bread. Mr. Hamilton had his faults, but starving his slaves was not one of them. He gave food in abundance, and of excellent quality. In Mr. Hamilton's cook — Aunt Mary — I found a generous and considerate friend. She never allowed me to go there without giving me bread enough to make good the deficiencies of a day or two. Master Thomas at last resolved to endure my behavior no longer; he could keep neither me nor his horse, we liked so well to be at his father-in-law's farm. I had lived with him nearly nine months and he had given me a number of severe whippings, without any visible improvement in my character or conduct, and now he was resolved to put me out, as he said, " *to be broken.*" There was, in the Bay-side, very near the camp-ground where my master received his religious impressions, a man named Edward Covey, who enjoyed the reputation of being a first rate hand at breaking young negroes. This Covey was a poor man, a farm renter; and his reputation of being a good hand to break in slaves was of immense pecuniary advantage to him, since it enabled him to get his farm tilled with very little expense, compared with what it would have cost him otherwise. Some slaveholders thought it an advantage to let Mr. Covey have the government of their slaves a year or two, almost free of charge, for the sake of the excellent training they had under his management. Like some horse-breakers noted for their skill, who ride the best horses in the country without expense, Mr. Covey could have under him the most fiery bloods of the neighborhood, for the simple reward of returning them to their owners *well broken.* Added to the natural fitness of Mr. Covey for the duties of his profession, he was said " to enjoy religion," and he was as strict in the cultivation of piety as he was in the cultivation of his farm. I was made aware of these traits in his character by some one who had been under his hand, and while I could not look forward to going to him with any degree of pleasure, I was glad to get away from St. Michaels. I believed I should get enough to eat at Covey's, even if I suffered in other respects, and this to a hungry man is not a prospect to be regarded with indifference.

Chapter XV

COVEY, THE NEGRO BREAKER.

Journey to Covey's—Meditations by the way—Covey's house—Family —Awkwardness as a field hand—A cruel beating—Why given-Description of Covey—First attempt at driving oxen —Hair-breadth escape—Ox and man alike property—Hard labor more effective than the whip for breaking down the spirit—Cunnin'g and trickery of Covey—Family worship—Shocking and indecent contempt for chastity—Great metal agitation—Anguish beyond description.

THE morning of January 1, 1834, with its chilling wind and pinching frost, quite in harmony with the winter in my own mind, found me, with my little bundle of clothing on the end of a stick swung across my shoulder, on the main road bending my way towards Covey's, whither I had been imperiously ordered by Master Thomas. He had been as good as his word, and had committed me without reserve to the mastery of that hard man. Eight or ten years had now passed since I had been taken from my grandmother's cabin in Tuckahoe; and these years, for the most part, I had spent in Baltimore, where, as the reader has already seen, I was treated with comparative tenderness. I was now about to sound profounder depths in slave life. My new master was notorious for his fierce and savage disposition, and my only consolation in going to live with him, was the certainty of finding him precisely as represented by common fame. There was neither joy in my heart nor elasticity in my frame as I started for the tyrant's home. Starvation made me glad to leave Thomas Auld's, and the cruel lash made me dread to go to Covey's. Escape, however, was impossible; so, heavy and sad, I paced the seven miles which lay between his house and St. Michaels, *thinking* much by the solitary way, of my adverse condition. But *thinking* was all I could do. Like a fish in a net, allowed to play for a time, I was now drawn rapidly to the shore and secured at all points. " I am," thought I, " but the sport of a power which makes no account, either of my welfare or of my happiness. By a law which I can comprehend, but cannot evade or resist, I am ruthlessly snatched from the hearth of a fond grandmother and hurried away to the home of a mysterious old master; again I am removed from there to a master in Baltimore; thence am I snatched away to the eastern shore to be valued with the beasts of the field, and with them divided and set apart for a possessor; then I am sent back to Baltimore, and by the time I have formed new attachments and have begun to hope that no more rude shocks shall touch me, a difference arises between brothers, and I am again broken up and sent to St. Michaels; and now from the latter place I am footing my way to the home of another master, where, I am given to understand, like a wild young working animal I am to he broken to the yoke of a bitter and life-long bondage." With thoughts and reflections like these I came in sight of a small wood-colored building, about a mile from the main road, and which, from the description I had received at starting, I easily recognized as my new home. The Chesapeake bay, upon the jutting banks of which the little wood-colored house was standing, white with foam raised by the heavy northwest wind; Poplar Island, covered with a thick black pine forest, standing out amid this half ocean; and Keat Point, stretching its sandy, desert-like shores out into the foam-crested bay, were all in sight, and served to deepen the wild and desolate scene.

The good clothes I had brought with me from Baltimore were now worn thin, and had not been replaced; for Master Thomas was as little careful to provide against cold as against hunger. Met here by a north wind sweeping through an open space of forty miles, I was glad to make any port, and, therefore, I speedily pressed on to the wood-colored house. The family consisted of Mr. and Mrs. Covey; Mrs. Kemp (a broken-backed woman), sister to Mrs. Covey ; William Hughes, cousin to Mr. Covey; Caroline, the cook; Bill Smith, a hired man, and myself. Bill Smith, Bill Hughes, and myself were the working force of the farm, which comprised three or four hundred acres. I was now for the first time in my life to be a field-hand; and in my new employment I found myself even more awkward than a green country boy may be supposed to be upon his first entrance into the bewildering scenes of city life. My awkwardness gave me much trouble. Strange and unnatural as it may seem, I had been in my *new* home but three days before Mr. Covey (my brother in the Methodist church,) gave me a bitter foretaste of what was in reserve for me. I presume he thought that, since he had but a single year in which to complete his work, the sooner he began the better. Perhaps he thought that by coming to blows at once we should mutually better understand our relations to each other. But to whatever motive, direct or indirect, the cause may be referred, I had not been in his possession three whole days before he subjected me to a most brutal chastisement. Under his heavy blows blood flowed freely, and wales were left on my back as large as my little finger. The sores from this flogging continued for weeks, for they were kept open by the rough and coarse cloth which I wore for shirting. The occasion and details of this first chapter of my experience as a field-hand must be told, that the reader may see how unreasonable, as well as how cruel, my new Master Covey was. The whole thing I found to be characteristic of the man, and I was probably treated no worse by him than had been scores of lads previously committed to him for reasons, similar to those which induced my master to place me with him. But here are the facts connected with the affair, precisely as they occurred.

On one of the coldest mornings of the whole month of January, 1834, I was ordered at daybreak to get a load of wood, from a forest about two miles from the house. In order to perform this work, Mr. Covey gave me a pair of unbroken oxen,for it seemed that his breaking abilities had not been turned in that direction. In due form, and with all proper ceremony, I was introduced to this huge yoke of unbroken oxen, and was carefully made to understand which was " Buck," and which was "Darby,"—which was the " in hand" ox, and which was the " off hand." The master of this important ceremony was no less a person than Mr. Covey himself, and the introduction was the first of the kind I had ever had.

My life, hitherto, had been quite away from horned cattle, and I had no knowledge of the art of managing them. What was meant by the " in ox," as against the "off ox," when both were equally fastened to one cart, and under one yoke, I could not very easily divine; and the difference implied by the names, and the peculiar duties of each, were alike *Greek* to me. Why was not the "off ox" called the "in ox?" Where and what is the reason for this distinction in names, when there is none in the things themselves ? After initiating me into the use of the "whoa," "back," "gee," "hither,"—the entire language spoken between oxen and driver,—Mr. Covey took a rope about ten feet long and one inch thick, and placed one end of it around the horns of the "in hand ox," and gave the other end to me, telling me that if the oxen started to run away (as the scamp knew they would), I must hold on to the rope and stop them. I need not tell any one who is acquainted with either the strength or the disposition of an untamed ox, that this order was about as unreasonable as a command to shoulder a mad bull. I had never before driven oxen and I was as awkward a driver as it is possible to conceive. I could not plead my ignorance to Mr. Covey. There was that in his manner which forbade any reply. Cold, distant, morose, with a face wearing all the marks of captious pride and malicious sternness, he repelled all advances. He was not a large man—not more than five feet ten inches in height, I should think; short-necked, round-shouldered, of quick and wiry motion, of thin and wolfish visage, with a pair of small, greenish-gray eyes, set well back under a forehead without dignity, and which were constantly in motion, expressing his passions rather than his thoughts, in sight, but denying them utterance in words. The creature presented an appearance altogether ferocious and sinister, disagreeable and forbidding, in the extreme. When he spoke, it was from the corner of his mouth, and in a sort of light growl like that of a dog when an attempt is made to take a bone from him. I already believed him a worse fellow than he had been represented to be. With his directions, and without stopping to question, I started for the woods, quite anxious to perform in a creditable manner, my first exploit in driving. The distance from the house to the wood's gate — a full mile, I should think — was passed over with little difficulty: for, although the animals ran, I was fleet enough in the open field to keep pace with them, especially as they pulled me along at the end of the rope; but on reaching the woods, I was speedily thrown into a distressing plight. The animals took fright, and started off ferociously into the woods, carrying the cart full tilt against trees, over stumps, and dashing from side to side in a manner altogether frightful. As I held the rope I expected every moment to be crushed between the cart and the huge trees, among which they were so furiously dashing. After running thus for several minutes, my oxen were finally brought to a stand, by a tree, against which they dashed themselves with great violence, upset-ting the cart, and entangling themselves among sundry young saplings. By the shock the body of the cart was flung in one direction and the wheels and tongue in another, and all in the greatest confusion. There I was, all alone in a thick wood to which I was a stranger; my cart upset and shattered, my oxen, wild and enraged, were entangled, and I, poor soul, was but a green hand to set all this disorder right. I knew no more of oxen than the ox-driver is supposed to know of wisdom.

After standing a few minutes, surveying the damage, and not without a presentiment that this trouble would draw after it others, even more distressing, I took one end of the cart-body and, by an extra outlay of strength, I lifted it toward the axle-tree, from which it had been violently flung. After much pulling and straining, I succeeded in getting the body of the cart in its place. This was an important step out of the difficulty, and its performance increased my courage for the work which remained to be done. The cart was provided with an ax, a tool with which I had become pretty well acquainted in the ship-yard at Baltimore. With this I cut down the saplings by which my oxen were entangled, and again pursued my journey, with my heart in my mouth, lest the oxen should again take it into their senseless heads to cut up a caper. But their spree was over for the present, and the rascals now moved off as soberly as though their behavior had been natural and exemplary. On reaching the part of the forest where I had, the day before, been chopping wood, I filled the cart with a heavy load, as a security against another runaway. But the neck of an ox is equal in strength to iron. It defies ordinary burdens. Tame and docile to a proverb, when *well* trained, when but half broken to the yoke, the ox is the most sullen and intractable of animals. I saw in my own situation several points of similarity with that of the oxen. They were property; so was I. Covey was to break me—I was to break them. Break and be broken was the order

Half of the day was already gone and I had not yet turned my face homeward. It required only two days' experience and observation to teach me that no such apparent waste of time would be lightly overlooked by Covey. I therefore hurried toward home; but in reaching the lane gate I met the crowning disaster of the day. This gate was a fair specimen of southern handicraft. There were two huge posts eighteen inches in diameter, rough hewed and square, and the heavy gate was so hung on one of these that it opened only about half the proper distance. On arriving here it was necessary for me to let go the end of the rope on the horns of the " in-hand ox"; and as soon as the gate was open and I let go of it to get the rope again, off went my oxen, full tilt; making nothing of their load, as, catching the huge gate between the wheel and the cart-body, they literally crushed it to splinters and came within only a few inches of subjecting me to a similar catastrophe, for I was just in advance of the wheel when it struck the left gatepost. With these two hair-breadth escapes I thought I could successfully explain to Mr. Covey the delay and avert punishment—I was not without a faint hope of being commended for the stern resolution which I had displayed in accomplishing the difficult task—a task which I afterwards learned even Covey himself would not have undertaken without first driving the oxen for some time in the open field, preparatory to their going to the woods. But in this hope I was disappointed. On coming to him his countenance assumed an aspect of rigid displeasure, and as I gave him a history of the casualties of my trip, his wolfish face, with his greenish eyes, became intensely ferocious. " Go back to the woods again," he said, muttering something else about wasting time. I hastily obeyed, but I had not gone far on my way when I saw him coming after me. My oxen now behaved themselves with singular propriety, contrasting their present conduct to my representation of their former antics. I almost wished, now that Covey was coming, they *would* do something in keeping with the character I had given them; but no, they had already had their spree, and they could afford now to be extra good, readily obeying orders, and seeming to understand them quite as well as I did myself. On reaching the woods, my tormenter, who seemed all the time to be remarking to himself upon the good behavior of the oxen, came up to me and ordered me to stop the cart, accompanying the same with the threat that he would now teach me how to break gates and idle away my time when he sent me to the woods. Suiting the action to the words, Covey paced off, in his own wiry fashion, to a large black gum tree, the young shoots of which are generally used for *ox-goads,* they being exceedingly tough. Three of these *goads,* from four to six feet long, he cut off and trimmed up with his large jack-knife. This done, he ordered me to take oil' my clothes. To this unreasonable order I made no reply, but in my apparent unconsciousness and inattention to this command I indicated very plainly a stern determination to do no such thing. " If you will beat me," thought I, " you shall do so over my clothes." After many threats, which made no

124

impression upon me, he rushed at me with something of the savage fierceness of a wolf, tore off the few and thinly worn clothes I had on, and proceeded to wear out on my back the heavy goads which he-had cut from the gum tree. This flogging was the first of a series of floggings, and though very severe, it was less so than many which came after it, and these for offences far lighter than the gate-breaking.

I remained with Mr. Covey one year (I cannot say I *lived* with him, and during the first six months that I was there I was whipped, either with sticks or cow-skins, every week. Aching bones and a sore back were my constant companions. Frequent as the lash was used, Mr. Covey thought less of it as a means of breaking down my spirit than that of hard and continued labor. He worked me steadily up to the point of my powers of endurance. From the dawn of day in the morning till the darkness was complete in the evening, I was kept hard at work in the field or the woods. At certain seasons of the year we were all kept in the field till eleven and twelve o'clock at night. At these times Covey would attend us in the field and urge us on with words or blows, as it seemed best to him. He had in his life been an overseer, and he well understood the business of slave-driving. There was no deceiving him. He knew just what a man or boy could do, and he held both to strict account. When he pleased he would work himself like a very Turk, making everything fly before him. It was, however, scarcely necessary for Mr. Covey to be really present in the field to have his work go on industriously. He had the faculty of making us feel that he was always present. By a series of adroitly managed surprises which he practiced, I was prepared to expect him at any moment. His plan was never to approach in an open, manly and direct manner the spot where his hands were at work. No thief was ever more artful in his devices than this man Covey. He would creep and crawl in ditches and gullies, hide behind stumps and bushes, and practice so much of the cunning of the serpent, that Bill Smith and I, between ourselves, never called him by any other name than " the snake." We fancied that in his eyes and his gait we could see a snakish resemblance. One-half of his proficiency in the art of negro-breaking consisted, I should think, in this species of cunning. We were never secure. He could see or hear us nearly all the time. He was, to us, behind every stump, tree, bush, and fence on the plantation. He carried this kind of trickery so far that he would sometimes mount his horse and make believe he was going to St. Michaels, and in thirty minutes afterwards you might find his horse tied in the woods, and the snake-like Covey lying flat in the ditch with his head lifted above its edge, or in a fence-corner, watching every movement of the slaves. I have known him walk up to us and give us special orders as to our work in advance, as if he were leaving home with a view to being absent several days, and before he got half way to the house he would avail himself of our inattention to his movements to turn short on his heel, conceal himself behind a fence-corner or a tree, and watch us until the going down of the sun. Mean and contemptible as is all this, it is in keeping with the character which the life of a slaveholder was calculated to produce. There was no earthly inducement in the slave's condition to incite him to labor faithfully. The fear of punishment was the sole motive of any sort of industry with him. Knowing this fact as the slaveholder did, and judging the slave by himself, he naturally concluded that the slave would be idle whenever the cause for this fear was absent. Hence all sorts of petty deceptions were practiced to inspire fear.

But with Mr. Covey trickery was natural. Everything in the shape of learning or religion which he possessed was made to conform to this semi-lying propensity. He did not seem conscious that the practice had anything unmanly, base or contemptible about it. It was with him a part of an important system essential to the relation of master and slave. I thought I saw, in his very religious devotions, this controlling element of his character. A long prayer at night made up for a short prayer in the morning, and few men could seem more devotional than he when he had nothing else to do.

Mr. Covey was not content with the cold style of family worship adopted in the cold latitudes, which begin and end with a simple prayer. No! the voice of praise as well as of prayer must be heard in his house night and morning. At first I was called upon to bear some part in these exercises; but the repeated floggings given me turned the whole thing into mockery. He was a poor singer and relied mainly upon me for raising the hymn for the family, and when I failed to do so he was thrown into much confusion. I do not think he ever abused me on account of these vexations. His religion was a thing altogether apart from his worldly concerns. He knew nothing of it as a holy principle directing and controlling his daily life and making the latter conform to the requirements of the gospel. One or two facts will illustrate his character better than a volume of generalities.

I have already implied that *Mr.* Edward Covey was a poor man. He was, in fact, just commencing to lay the foundation of his fortune, as fortune was regarded in a slave state. The first condition of wealth and respectability there being the ownership of human property, every nerve was strained by the poor man to obtain it, with little regard sometimes as to the means. In pursuit of this object, pious as Mr. Covey was, he proved himself as unscrupulous and base as the worst of his neighbors. In the beginning he was only able—as he said—" to buy one slave;" and scandalous and shocking as is the fact, he boasted that he bought her simply " as a breeder." But the worst of this is not told in this naked statement. This young woman (Caroline was her name) was virtually compelled by Covey to abandon herself to the object for which he had purchased her; and the result was the birth of twins at the end of the year. At this addition to his human stock Covey and his wife were ecstatic with joy. No one dreamed of reproaching the woman or of finding fault with the hired man, Bill Smith, the father of the children, for Mr. Covey himself had locked the two up together every night, thus inviting the result.

But I will pursue this revolting subject no farther. No better illustration of the unchaste, demoralizing, and de-basing character of slavery can be found, than is furnished in the fact that this professedly Christian slaveholder, amidst all his prayers and hymns, was shamelessly and boastfully encouraging and actually compelling, in his own house, undisguised and unmitigated fornication, as a means of increasing his stock. It was the *system* of slavery which made this allowable, and which no more condemned the slaveholder for buying a slave woman and devoting her to this life, than for buying a cow and raising stock from her, and the same rules were observed, with a view to increasing the number and quality of the one, as of the other.

If at any one time of my life, more than another, I was made to drink the bitterest dregs of slavery, that time was during the first six months of my stay with this man Covey. We worked all weathers. It was never too hot, or too cold; it could never rain, blow, snow, or hail too hard for us to work in the field. Work, work, work, was scarcely more the order of the day than of the night. The longest days were too short for him, and the shortest nights were too long for him. I was somewhat unmanageable at the first, but a few months of this discipline tamed me. Mr. Covey succeeded in *breaking* me—in body, soul, and spirit. My natural elasticity was crushed; my intellect languished; the disposition to read departed, the cheerful spark that lingered about my eye died out; the dark night of slavery closed in upon me, and behold a man transformed to a brute !

Sunday was my only leisure time. I spent this under some large tree, in a sort of beast-like stupor between sleeping and waking. At times I would rise up and a flash of energetic freedom would dart through my soul, accompanied with a faint beam of hope that flickered for a moment, and then vanished. I sank down again, mourning over my wretched condition. I was sometimes tempted to take my life and that of Covey, but was prevented by a combination of hope and fear. My sufferings, as I remember them now, seem like a dream rather than like a stern reality.

Our house stood within a few rods of the Chesapeake bay, whose broad bosom was ever white with sails from every quarter of the habitable globe. Those beautiful vessels, robed in white, and so delightful to the eyes of freemen, were to me so many shrouded ghosts, to terrify and torment me with thoughts of my wretched condition. I have often, in the deep stillness of a summer's Sabbath, stood all alone upon the banks of that noble bay, and traced, with saddened heart and tearful eye, the countless number of sails moving off to the mighty ocean. The sight of these always affected me powerfully. My thoughts would compel utterance ; and there, with no audience but the Almighty, I would pour out my soul's complaint in my rude way with an apostrophe to the moving multitude of ships.

"You are loosed from your moorings, and free. I am fast in my chains, and am a slave ! You move merrily before the gentle gale, and I sadly before the bloody whip. You are freedom's swift-winged angels, that fly around the world; I am confined in bonds of iron. O, that I were free! O, that I were on one of your gallant decks, and under your protecting wing! Alas! betwixt me and you the turbid waters roll. Go on, go on; O, that I could also go ! Could I but swim ! If I could fly ! O, why was I born a man, of whom to make a brute! The glad ship is gone. she hides in the dim distance. I am left in the hell of unending slavery. O, God, save me ! God, deliver me! Let me be free !—Is there any God ? Why am I a slave ? I will run away. I will not stand it. Get caught or get clear, I'll try it. I had as well die with ague as with fever. I have only one life to lose. I had as well be killed running as die standing. Only think of it: one hundred miles north, and I am free! Try it ? Yes! God helping me, I will. It cannot be that I shall live and die a slave. I will take to the water. This very bay shall yet bear me into freedom. The steamboats steer in a northeast course from North Point; I will do the same ; and when I get to the head of the bay, I will turn my canoe adrift, and walk straight through Delaware into Pennsylvania. When I get there I shall not be required to have a pass: I will travel there without being disturbed. Let but the first opportunity offer, and come what will, I am off. Meanwhile I will try to bear the yoke. I am not the only slave in the world. Why should I fret? I can bear as much as any of them. Besides I am but a boy yet, and all boys are bound out to some one. It may be that my misery in slavery will only increase my happiness when I get free. There is a better day coming."

I shall never be able to narrate half the mental experience through which it was my lot to pass, during my stay at Covey's. I was completely wrecked, changed, and bewildered; goaded almost to madness at one time, and at another reconciling myself to my wretched condition. All the kindness I had received at Baltimore, all my former hopes and aspirations for usefulness in the world, and even the happy moments spent in the exercises of religion, contrasted with my then present lot, served but to increase my anguish.

I suffered bodily as well as mentally. I had neither sufficient time in which to eat, or to sleep, except on Sundays. The over-work, and the brutal chastisements of which I was the victim, combined with that ever-gnawing and soul-devouring thought—" *I am a slave—a slave for life—a slave with no rational ground to hope for freedom* "—rendered me a living embodiment of mental and physical wretchedness.

Chapter XVI.

ANOTHER PRESSURE OF THE TYRANT'S VISE.

Experience at Covey's summed up—First six months severer than the remaining six—Preliminaries to the change—Reasons for narrating the circumstances—Scene in the treading-yard—Author taken ill— Escapes to St. Michaels—The pursuit—Suffering in the woods— Talk with Master Thomas—His beating—Driven back to Covey's— The slaves never sick—Natural to expect them to feign sickness— Laziness of slaveholders.

THE reader has but to repeat, in his mind, once a week the scene in the woods, where Covey subjected me to his merciless lash, to have a true idea of my bitter experience, during the first six months of the breaking process through which he carried me. I have no heart to repeat each separate transaction. Such a narration would fill a volume much larger than the present one. I aim only to give the reader a truthful impression of my slave-life, without unnecessarily affecting him with harrowing details.

As I have intimated that my hardships were much greater during the first six months of my stay at Covey's than during the remainder of the year, and as the change in my condition was owing to causes which may help the reader to a better understanding of human nature, when subjected to the terrible extremities of slavery, I will narrate the circumstances of this change, although I may seem thereby to applaud my own courage.

You have, dear reader, seen me humbled, degraded, broken down, enslaved, and brutalized; and you understand how it was done; now let us see the converse of all this, and how it was brought about; and this will take us through the year 1834.

On one of the hottest days of the month of August of the year just mentioned, had the reader been passing through Covey's farm, he might have seen me at work in what was called the "treading-yard"—a yard upon which wheat was trodden out from the straw by the horses' feet. I was there at work feeding the "fan," or rather bringing wheat to the fan, while Bill Smith was feeding. Our force consisted of Bill Hughes, Bill Smith, and a slave by the name of Eli, the latter having been hired for the occasion. The work was simple, and required strength and activity, rather than any skill or intelligence; and yet to one entirely unused to such work, it came very hard. The heat was intense and overpowering, and there was much hurry to get the wheat trodden out that day, through the fan; since if that work was done an hour before sundown, the hands would have, according to a promise of Covey, that hour added to their night's rest. I was not behind any of them in the wish to complete the day's work before sundown, and hence I struggled with all my might to get it forward. The promise of one hour's repose on a week day was sufficient to quicken my pace, and to spur me on to extra endeavor. Besides, we had all planned to go fishing, and I certainly wished to have a hand in that. But I was disappointed, and the day turned out to be one of the bitterest I ever experienced. About three o'clock, while the sun was pouring down his burning rays, and not a breeze was stirring, I broke down; my strength failed me; I was seized with a violent aching of the head, attended with extreme dizziness, and trembling in every limb. Finding what was coming, and feeling that it would never do to stop work, I nerved myself up and staggered on, until I fell by the side of the wheat fan, with a feeling that the earth had fallen in upon me. This brought the entire work to a dead stand. There was work for four: each one had his part to perform, and each part depended on the other, so that when one stopped, all were compelled to stop. Covey, who had become my dread, was at the house, about a hundred yards from where I was fanning, and instantly, upon hearing the fan stop, he came down to the treading-yard to inquire into the cause of the interruption. Bill Smith told him that I was sick and unable longer to bring wheat to the fan.

I had by this time crawled away in the shade, under the side of a post-and-rail fence, and was exceedingly ill. The intense heat of the sun, the heavy dust rising from the fan, and the stooping to take up the wheat from the yard, together with the hurrying to get through, had caused a rush of blood to my head. In this condition Covey, finding out where I was, came to me, and after standing over me a while asked what the matter was. I told him as well as 1 could, for it was with difficulty that I could speak. He gave me a savage kick in the side which jarred my whole frame, and commanded me to get up. The monster had obtained complete control over me, and if he had commanded me to do any possible thing I should, in my then state of mind, have endeavored to comply. I made an effort to rise, but fell back in the attempt before gaining my feet. He gave me another heavy kick, and again told me to rise. I again tried, and succeeded in standing up; but upon stooping to get the tub with which I was feeding the fan I again staggered and fell to the ground. I must have so fallen had I been sure that a hundred bullets would have pierced me through as the consequence. While down in this sad condition, and perfectly helpless, the merciless negro-breaker took up the hickory slab with which Hughes had been striking off the wheat to a level with the sides of the half-bushel measure,(a very hard weapon), and,with the edge of it, he dealt me a heavy blow on my head which made a large gash, and caused the blood to run freely, saying at the same time, " If you have got the headache I'll cure you." This done, he ordered me again to rise, but I made no effort to do so, for I had now made up my mind that it was useless and that the heartless villain might do his worst. He could but kill me and that might put me out of my misery. Finding me unable to rise, or rather despairing of my doing so, Covey left me, with a view to getting on with the work without me. I was bleeding very freely, and my face was soon covered with my warm blood. Cruel and merciless as was the motive that dealt that blow, the wound was a fortunate one for me. Bleeding was never more efficacious. The pain in my head speedily abated, and I was soon able to rise. Covey had, as I have said, left me to my fate, and the question was, shall I return to my work, or shall I find my way to St. Michaels and make Capt. Auld acquainted with the atrocious cruelty of his brother Covey, and beseech him to get me another master? Remembering the object he had in view in placing me under the management of Covey, and further, his cruel treatment of my poor crippled cousin Henny, and his meanness in the matter of feeding and clothing his slaves, there was little ground to hope for a favorable reception at the hands of Capt. Thomas Auld. Nevertheless, I resolved to go straight to him, thinking that, if not animated by motives of humanity, he might be induced to interfere on my behalf from selfish considerations. "He cannot," I thought, "allow his property to be thus bruised and battered, marred and defaced, and I will go to him about the matter." In order to get to St. Michaels by the most favorable and direct road I must walk seven miles, and this, in my sad condition, was no easy performance. I had already lost much blood, I was exhausted by over-exertion, my sides were sore from the heavy blows planted there by the stout boots of Mr. Covey, and I was in every way in an unfavorable plight for the journey. I however watched my chance while the cruel and cunning Covey was looking in an opposite direction, and started off across the field for St. Michaels. This was a daring step. If it failed it would only exasperate Covey and increase during the remainder of my term of service under him, the rigors of my bondage. But the step was taken and I must go forward. I succeeded in getting nearly half way across the broad field toward the woods, when Covey observed me. I was still bleeding and the exertion of running had started the blood afresh. " *Come back ! Come back !*" he vociferated, with threats of what he would do if I did not instantly return. But, disregarding his calls and threats, I pressed on toward the woods as fast as my feeble state would allow. Seeing no signs of my stopping,he caused his horse to be brought out and saddled, as if he intended to pursue me. The race was now to be an unequal one, and thinking I might be overhauled by him if I kept the main road, I walked nearly the whole distance in the woods, keeping far enough from the road to avoid detection and pursuit. But I had not gone far before my little strength again failed me, and I was obliged to lie down. The blood was still oozing from the wound in my head, and for a time I suffered more than I can describe. There I was in the deep woods, sick and emaciated, bleeding and almost bloodless, and pursued by a wretch whose character for revolting cruelty beggars all opprobrious speech. I was not without the fear of bleeding to death. The thought of dying all alone in the woods, and of being torn in pieces by the buzzards, had not yet been rendered tolerable by my many troubles and hardships, and I was glad when the shade of the trees and the cool evening breeze combined with my matted hair to stop the flow of blood. After lying there about three-quarters of an hour, brooding over the singular and mournful lot to which I was doomed, my mind passing over the whole scale or circle of belief and unbelief, from faith in the overruling Providence of God, to the blackest atheism, I again took up my journey toward St. Michaels, more weary and sad than on the morning when I left Thomas Anld's for the home of Covey. I was bare-footed, bare-headed, and in my shirt-sleeves. The way was through briers and bogs, and I tore my feet often during the journey. I was full five hours in going the seven or eight miles ; partly because of the difficulties of the way, and partly because of the feebleness induced by my illness, bruises, and loss of blood.

On gaining my master's store, I presented an appearance of wretchedness and woe calculated to move any but a heart of stone. From the crown of my head to the sole of my feet, there were marks of blood. My hair was all clotted with dust and blood, and the back of my shirt was literally stiff with the same. Briers and thorns had scarred and torn my feet and legs. Had I escaped from a den of tigers, I could not have looked worse. In this plight I appeared before my professedly *Christian* master, humbly to invoke the interposition of his power and authority, to protect me from further abuse and violence. During the latter part of my tedious journey I had begun to hope that my master would now show himself in a nobler light I had before seen him. But I was disappointed. I had jumped from a sinking ship into the sea. I had fled from a tiger to something worse. I told him as well as I could, all the circumstances; how I was endeavoring to please Covey; how hard I was at work in the present instance; how unwillingly I sank down under the heat, toil, and pain; the brutal manner in which Covey had kicked me in the side, the gash cut in my head; my hesitation about troubling him (Capt. Auld) with complaints; but that now I felt it would not be best longer to conceal from him the outrages committed from time to time upon me. At first Master Thomas seemed somewhat affected by the story of my wrongs, but he soon repressed whatever feeling he may have had, and became as cold and hard as iron. It was impossible, *at first,* as I stood before him, to seem indifferent. I distinctly saw his human nature asserting its conviction against the slave system, which made cases like mine *possible ;* but, as I have said, humanity fell before the systematic tyranny of slavery. He first walked the floor, apparently much agitated by my story, and the spectacle I presented; but soon it was *his* turn to talk. He began moderately by finding excuses for Covey, and ended with a full justification of him, and a passionate condemnation of me. He had no doubt I deserved the flogging. He did not believe I was sick; I was only endeavoring to get rid of work. My dizziness was laziness, and Covey did right to flog me as he had done. After thus fairly annihilating me, and arousing himself by his eloquence, he fiercely demanded what I wished *Mm* to do in the case! With such a knock-down to all my hopes, and feeling as I did my entire subjection to his power, I had very little heart to reply. I must not assert my innocence of the allegations he had piled up against me, for that would be impudence. The guilt of a slave was always and everywhere presumed, and the innocence of the slaveholder, or employer, was always asserted. The word of the slave against this presumption was generally treated as impudence, worthy of punishment. " Do you dare to contradict me, you rascal ?" was a final silencer of counter-statements from the lips of a slave. Calming down a little, in view of my silence and hesitation, and perhaps a little touched at my forlorn and miserable appearance, he inquired again, what I wanted him to do? Thus invited a second time, I told him I wished him to allow me to get a new home, and to find a new master; that as sure as I went back to live again with Mr. Covey, I should be killed by him; that he would never forgive my coming home with complaints; that since I had lived with him he had almost crushed my spirit, and I believed he would ruin me for future service and that my life was not safe in his hands. This Master Thomas *(my brother in the church)* regarded as " nonsense." There was no danger that Mr. Covey would kill me; he was a good man, industrious and religious, and he would not think of removing me from that home; " besides," said he—and this I found was the most distressing thought of all to him—"if you should leave Covey now that your year is but half expired, I should lose your wages for the entire year. You belong to Mr. Covey for one year, and you *must go hack* to him, come what will; and you must not trouble me with any more stories; and if you don't go immediately home, I'll get hold of you myself." This was just what I expected when I found he had *prejudged* the case against me. " But, sir," I said, " I am sick and tired, and I *cannot* get home to-night." At this he somewhat relented, and finally allowed me to stay the night, but said I must be off early in the morning, and concluded his directions by making me swallow a huge dose of Epsom salts, which was about the only medicine ever administered to slaves. It was quite natural for Master Thomas to presume I was feigning sickness to escape work, for he probably thought that were he in the place of a slave, with no wages for his work, no praise for well-doing, no motive for toil but the lash, he would try every possible scheme by which to escape labor. I say I have no doubt of this; the reason is, that there were not, under the whole heavens, a set of men who cultivated such a dread of labor as did the slaveholders. The charge of laziness against the slaves was ever on their lips and was the standing apology for every species of cruelty and brutality. These men did indeed literally " bind heavy burdens, grievous to be borne, and laid them upon men's shoulders, but they themselves would not move them with one of their fingers."

Chapter XVII.

THE LAST FLOGGING.

A sleepless night—Return to Covey's—Punished by him—
The chase defeated—Vengeance postponed—Musings in
the woods—The alternative—Deplorable spectacle—Night
in the woods—Expected attack—Accosted by Sandy—A
friend, not a master—Sandy's hospitality—The ash-cake
supper—Interview with Sandy—His advice —Sandy a
conjuror as well as a Christian—The magic root— Strange
meeting with Covey—His manner—Covey's Sunday face—
Author's defensive resolve—The fight—The victory, and its
results.

SLEEP does not always come to the relief of the
weary in body, and broken in spirit; especially is it so
when past troubles only foreshadow coming disasters. My
last hope had been extinguished. My master, who I did not
venture to hope would protect me *as a* MAN, had now refused
to protect me as *his property,* and had cast me back, covered
with reproaches and bruises, into the hands of one who was
a stranger to that mercy which is the soul of the religion he
professed. May the reader never know what it is to spend
such a night as to me was that which heralded my return
to the den of horrors from which I had made a temporary
escape.

I remained—sleep I did not—all night at St. Michaels,
and in the morning (Saturday) I started off, obedient to the
order of Master Thomas, feeling that I had no friend on earth,
and doubting if I had one in heaven. I reached Covey's about

nine o'clock; and just as I stepped into the field, before I had reached the house, true to his snakish habits, Covey darted out at me from a fence corner, in which he had secreted himself for the purpose of securing me. He was provided with a cowskin and a rope, and he evidently intended to *tie me up,* and wreak his vengeance on me to the fullest extent. I should have been an easy prey had he succeeded in getting his hands upon me, for I had taken no refreshment since noon on Friday; and this, with the other trying circumstances, had greatly reduced my strength. I, however, darted back into the woods before the ferocious hound could reach me, and buried myself in a thicket, where he lost sight of me. The cornfield afforded me shelter in getting to the woods. But for the tall corn, Covey would have overtaken me, and made me his captive. He was much chagrined that he did not, and gave up the chase very reluctantly, as I could see by his angry movements, as he returned to the house.

For a little time I was clear of Covey and his lash. I was in the wood, buried in its somber gloom and hushed in its solemn silence; hidden from all human eyes ; shut in with nature and with nature's God, and absent from all human contrivances. Here was a good place to pray ; to pray for help, for deliverance—a prayer I had often before made. But how could I pray ? Covey could pray—Capt. Auld could pray. I would fain pray ; but doubts arising, partly from my neglect of the means of grace and partly from the sham religion which everywhere prevailed, there was awakened in my mind a distrust of all religion and the conviction that prayers were unavailing and delusive.

Life in itself had almost become burdensome to me. All my outward relations were against me. I must stay here and starve, or go home to Covey's and have my flesh torn to pieces and my spirit humbled under his cruel lash. These were the alternatives before me. The day was long and irksome. I was weak from the toils of the previous day and from want of food and sleep, and I had been so little concerned about my appearance that I had not yet washed the blood from my garments. I was an object of horror, even to myself. Life in Baltimore, when most oppressive, was a paradise to this. What had I done, what had my parents done, that such a life as this should be mine? That day, in the woods, I would have exchanged my manhood for the brutehood of an ox. Night came. I was still in the woods, and still unresolved what to do. Hunger had not yet pinched me to the point of going home, and I laid myself down in the leaves to rest; for I had been watching for hunters all day, but not being molested by them during the day, I. expected no disturbance from them during the night. I had come to the conclusion that Covey relied upon hunger to drive me home, and in this I was quite correct, for he made no effort to catch me after the morning.

During the night I heard the step of a man in the woods. He was coming toward the place where I lay. *A* person lying still in the woods in the day-time has the advantage over one walking, and this advantage is much greater at night. I was not able to engage in a physical struggle, and I had recourse to the common resort of the weak. I hid myself in the leaves to prevent discovery. But as the night rambler in the woods drew nearer I found him to be *a friend,* not an enemy; a slave of Mr. William Groomes of Easton, a kind-hearted fellow named "Sandy." Sandy lived that year with Mr. Kemp, about four miles from St. Michaels. He, like myself, had been hired out, but unlike myself had not been hired out to be broken. He was the husband of a free woman who lived in the lower part of "Poppie Neck," and he was now on his way through the woods to see her and to spend the Sabbath with her.

As soon as I had ascertained that the disturber of my solitude was not an enemy, but the good-hearted Sandy, —a man as famous among the slaves of the neighbor hood for his good nature as for his good sense—I came out from my hiding-place and made myself known to him. I explained the circumstances of the past two days which had driven me to the woods, and he deeply compassionated my distress. It was a bold thing for him to shelter me, and I could not ask him to do so, for had I been found in his hut he would have suffered the penalty of thirty-nine lashes on his bare back, if not something worse. But Sandy was too generous to permit the fear of punishment to prevent his relieving a brother bond man from hunger and exposure, and therefore, on his own motion, accompanied him home to his wife— for the house and lot were hers, as she was a free woman. It was about midnight, but his wife was called up, a lire was made, some Indian meal was soon mixed with salt and water, and an ash-cake was baked in a hurry, to relieve my hunger. Sandy's wife was not behind him in kindness ; both seemed to esteem it a privilege to succor me, for although I was hated by Covey and by my master I was loved by the colored people, because they thought I was hated for my knowledge, and persecuted because I was feared. I was the only slave in that region who could read or write. There had been one other man, belonging to Mr. Hugh Hamilton, who could read, but he, poor fellow, had, shortly after coming into the neighborhood, been sold off to the far south. I saw him in the cart, to be carried to Easton for sale, ironed and pinioned like a yearling for the slaughter. My knowledge was now the pride of my brother slaves, and no doubt Sandy felt on that account something of the general interest in me. The supper was soon ready, and though over the sea I have since feasted with honorables, lord mayors and aldermen, my supper on ash-cake and cold water, with Sandy, was the meal of all my life most sweet to my taste and now most vivid to my memory.

Supper over, Sandy and I went into a discussion of what was *possible* for me, under the perils and hardships which overshadowed my path. The question was, must I go back to Covey, or must I attempt to run away ? Upon a careful survey the latter was found to be impossible ; for I was on a narrow neck of land, every avenue from which would bring me in sight of pursuers. There was Chesapeake Bay to the right, and "Pot-pie" river to the left, and St. Michaels and its neighborhood occupied the only space through which there was any retreat.

I found Sandy an old adviser. He was not only a religious man, but he professed to believe in a system for which I have no name. He was a genuine African, and had inherited some of the so-called magical powers said to be possessed by the eastern nations. He told me that he could help me; that in those very woods there was an herb which in the morning might be found, possessing all the powers required for my protection (I put his words in my own language), and that if I would take his advice he would procure me the root of the herb of which he spoke. He told me, further, that if I would take that root and wear it on my right side it would be impossible for Covey, to strike me a blow, and that, with this root about my person, no white man could whip me. He said he had carried it for years, and that he had fully tested its virtues. He had never received a blow from a slaveholder since he carried it, and he never expected to receive one, for he meant always to carry that root for protection. He knew Covey well, for Mrs. Covey was the daughter of Mrs. Kemp; and he (Sandy) had heard of the barbarous treatment to which I had been subjected, and he wanted to do something for me.

Now all this talk about the root was to me very absurd and ridiculous, if not positively sinful. I at first rejected the idea that the simple carrying a root on my right side (a root, by the way, over which I walked every time I went into the woods) could possess any such magic power as he ascribed to it, and I was, therefore, not disposed to cumber my pocket with it. I had a positive aversion to all pretenders to *"divination."* It was beneath one of my intelligence to countenance such dealings with the devil as this power implied. But with all my learning— it was really precious little—Sandy was more than a match for me. "My book-learning," he said, "had not kept Covey off me" (a powerful argument just then), and he entreated me, with flashing eyes, to try this. If it did me no good it could do me no harm, and it would cost me nothing any way. Sandy was so earnest and so confident of the good qualities of this weed that, to please him, I was induced to take it. He had been to me the good Samaritan, and had, almost providentially, found me and helped me when I could not help myself; how did I know but that the hand of the Lord was in it. With thoughts of this sort I took the roots from Sandy and put them in my right-hand pocket.

This was of course Sunday morning. Sandy now urged me to go home with all speed, and to walk up bravely to the house, as though nothing had happened. I saw in Sandy, with all his superstition, too deep an insight into human nature not to have some respect for his advice; and perhaps, too, a slight gleam or shadow of his superstition had fallen on me. At any rate, I started off toward Covey' directed. Having, the previous night, poured my griefs into Sandy's ears and enlisted him in my behalf, having made his wife a sharer in my sorrows, and having also become well refreshed by sleep and food, I moved off quite courageously toward the dreaded Covey's. Singularly enough, just as I entered the yard-gate I met him and his wife on their way to church, dressed in their Sunday best, and looking as smiling as angels.

His manner perfectly astonished me. There was something really benignant in his countenance. He spoke to me as never before, told me that the pigs had got into the lot and he wished me to go to drive them out; inquired how I was, and seemed an altered man. This extraordinary conduct really made me begin to think that Sandy's herb had more virtue in it than I, in my pride, had been willing to allow, and, had the day been other than Sunday, I should have attributed Covey's altered manner solely to the power of the root. I suspected, however, that the *Sabbath,* not the root, was the real explanation of the change. His religion hindered him from breaking the Sabbath, but not from breaking my skin on any other day than Sunday. He had more respect for the day than for the man for whom the day was mercifully given; for while he would cut and slash my body during the week, he would on Sunday teach me the value of my soul, and the way of life and salvation by Jesus Christ.

All went well with me till Monday morning; and then, whether the root had lost its virtue, or whether my tormentor had gone deeper into the black art than I had,(as was sometimes said of him), or whether he had obtained a special indulgence for his faithful Sunday's worship, it is not necessary for me to know or to inform the reader; but this much I may say, the pious and benignant smile which graced the face of Covey on *Sunday* wholly disappeared on *Monday.*

Long before daylight I was called up to go feed, rub, and curry the horses. I obeyed the call, as I should have done had it been made at an earlier hour, for I had brought my mind to a firm resolve during that Sunday's reflection to obey every order, however unreasonable, if it were possible, and if Mr. Covey should then undertake to beat me to defend and protect myself to the best of my ability. My religious views on the subject of resisting my master had suffered a serious shock by the savage persecution to which I had been subjected, and my hands were no longer tied by my religion. Master Thomas's indifference had severed the last link. I had backslidden from this point in the slaves' religious creed, and I soon had occasion to make my fallen state known to my Sunday-pious brother, Covey.

While I was obeying his order to feed and get the horses ready for the field, and when I was in the act of going up the stable-loft, for the purpose of throwing down some blades, Covey sneaked into the stable, in his peculiar way, and seizing me suddenly by the leg, he brought me to the stable-floor, giving my newly-mended body a terrible jar. I now forgot all about my *roots,* and remembered my pledge to stand up in my own defense. The brute was skillfully endeavoring to get a slip-knot on my legs, before I could draw up my feet. As soon as I found what he was up to, I gave a sudden spring (my two days' rest had been of much service to me) and by that means, no doubt, he was able to bring me to the floor so heavily. He was defeated in his plan of tying me. While down, he seemed to think that he had me very securely in his power. He little thought he was—as the rowdies say— "in" for a "rough and tumble" fight; but such was the fact. Whence came the daring spirit necessary to grapple with a man who, eight-and-forty hours before, could, with his slightest word, have made me tremble like a leaf in a storm, I do not know ; at any rate, I *was resolved to fight,* and what was better still, I actually was hard at it. The fighting madness had come upon me, and I found my strong fingers firmly attached to the throat of the tyrant, as heedless of consequences, at the moment, as if we stood as equals before the law. The very color of the man was forgotten. I felt supple as a cat, and was ready for him at every turn. Every blow of his was parried, though I dealt no blows in return. I was strictly on the *defensive,* preventing him from injuring me, rather than trying to injure him. I flung him on the ground several times when he meant to have hurled me there. I held him so firmly by the throat that his blood followed my nails. He held me, and I held him.

All was fair thus far, and the contest was about equal. My resistance was entirely unexpected and Covey was taken all aback by it. He trembled in every limb. ''Are you going to resist, you scoundrel?" said he. To which I returned a polite " Yes, sir," steadily gazing my interrogator in the eye, to meet the first approach or dawning of the blow which I expected my answer would call forth. But the conflict did not long remain equal. Covey soon cried lustily for help; not that I was obtaining any marked advantage over him, or was injuring him, but because he was gaining none over me, and was not able, single-handed, to conquer me. He called for his cousin Hughes to come to his assistance, and now the scene was changed. I was compelled to give blows, as well as to parry them, and since I was in any case to suffer for resistance, I felt (as the musty proverb goes) that I " might as well be hanged for an old sheep as a lamb." I was still defensive toward Covey, but aggressive toward Hughes, on whom, at his first approach, I dealt a blow which fairly sickened him. He went off, bending over with pain, and manifesting no disposition to come again within my reach. The poor fellow was in the act of trying to catch and tie my right hand, and while flattering himself with success, I gave him the kick which sent him staggering away in pain, at the same time that I held Covey with a firm hand.

Taken completely by surprise, Covey seemed to have lost his usual strength and coolness. He was frightened, and stood puffing and blowing, seemingly unable to command words or blows. When he saw that Hughes was standing half bent with pain, his courage quite gone, the cowardly tyrant asked if I meant to persist in my resistance." I told him I " *did mean to resist,* come what might; that I had been treated like a brute during the last six months, and that I should stand it no longer." With that he gave me a shake, and attempted to drag me toward a stick of wood that was lying just outside the stable-door. He meant to knock me down with it; but, just as he leaned over to get the stick, I seized him with both hands, by the collar, and with a vigorous and sudden snatch brought my assailant harmlessly, his full length, on the not over-clean ground, for we were now in the cow-yard. He had selected the place for the fight, and it was but right that he should have all the advantages of his own selection.

By this time Bill, the hired man, came home. He had been to Mr. Helmsley's to spend Sunday with his nomi-nal wife. Covey and I had been skirmishing from before daybreak till now. The sun was shooting his beams almost over the eastern woods, and we were still at it. I could not see where the matter was to terminate. He evidently was afraid to let me go, lest I should again make off to the woods, otherwise he would probably have obtained arms from the house to frighten me. Holding me, he called upon Bill to assist him. The scene here had something comic about it. Bill, who knew precisely what Covey wished him to do, affected ignorance, and pretended he did not know what to do. " What shall I do, Master Covey ?" said Bill. " Take hold of him! — take hold of him !" cried Covey. With a toss of his head, peculiar to Bill, he said : " Indeed, Master Covey, I want to go to work."

" *This is your work*" said Covey ; "take hold of him." Bill replied, with spirit: " My master hired me here to work, and not to help you whip Frederick."

It was my turn to speak. " Bill," said I, " don't put your hands on me." To which he replied: " My God, Frederick, I ain't goin' to tech ye" ; and Bill walked off,leaving Covey and myself to settle our differences as best we might.

But my present advantage was threatened when I saw Caroline (the slave woman of Covey) coming to the cow-yard to milk, for she was a powerful woman, and could have mastered me easily, exhausted as I was.

As soon as she came near, Covey attempted to rally her to his aid. Strangely and fortunately, Caroline was in no humor to take a hand in any such sport. We were all in open rebellion that morning. Caroline answered the command of her master to " take hold of me," precisely as Bill had done, but in her it was at far greater peril, for she was the slave of Covey, and he could do what he pleased with her. It was not so with Bill, and - Bill knew it. Samuel Harris, to whom Bill belonged, did not allow his slaves to be beaten unless they were guilty of some crime which the law would punish. But poor Caroline, like myself, was at the mercy of the merciless Covey, nor did she escape the dire effects of her refusal: he gave her several sharp blows.

At length (two hours had elapsed) the contest was given over. Letting go of me, puffing and blowing at a great rate, Covey said : "Now, you scoundrel, go to your work ; I would not have whipped you half so hard if you had not resisted." The fact was, he had not whipped me at all. He had not, in all the scuffle, drawn a single drop of blood from me. I had drawn blood from him, and should even without this satisfaction have been victorious, because my aim had not been to injure him, but to prevent his injuring me.

During the whole six months that I lived with Covey after this transaction, he never again laid the weight of his finger on me in anger. He would occasionally say he did not want to have to get hold of me again—a declaration which I had no difficulty in believing ; and I had a secret feeling which answered, " You had better not wish to get hold of me again, for you will be likely to come off worse in a second fight than you did in the first."

This battle with Mr. Covey, undignified as it was and as I fear my narration of it is, was the turning-point in my " life as a slave." It rekindled in my breast the smouldering embers of liberty. It brought up my Baltimore dreams and revived a sense of my own manhood. I was a changed being after that fight. I was nothing before ; I was a man now. It recalled to life my crushed self-respect, and my self-confidence, and inspired me with a renewed determination to be a free man. A man without force is without the essential dignity of humanity. Human nature is so constituted, that it cannot honor a helpless man, though it can pity him, and even this it cannot do long if signs of power do not arise.

He only can understand the effect of this combat on my spirit, who has himself incurred something, or hazarded something, in repelling the unjust and cruel aggressions of a tyrant. Covey was a tyrant and a cowardly one withal. After resisting him, I felt as I had never felt before. It was a resurrection from the dark and pestiferous tomb of slavery, to the heaven of comparative freedom. I was no longer a servile coward, trembling under the frown of a brother worm of the dust, but my long-cowed spirit was roused to an attitude of independence. I had reached the point at which I was not afraid to die. This spirit made me a freeman in fact, though I still remained a slave in form. When a slave cannot be flogged, he is more than half free. He has a domain as broad as his own manly heart to defend, and he is really "a power on earth." From this time until my escape from slavery, I was never fairly whipped. Several attempts were made, but they were always unsuccessful. Bruised I did get, but the instance I have described was the end of the brutification to which slavery had subjected me.

The reader may like to know why, after I had so grievously offended Mr. Covey, he did not have me taken in hand by the authorities ; indeed, why the law of Maryland, which assigned hanging to the slave who resisted his master, was not put in force against me, at any rate why I was not taken up, as was usual in such cases, and publicly whipped as an example to other slaves, and as a means of deterring me from again committing the same offence. I confess that the easy manner in which I got off was always a surprise to me, and even now I cannot fully explain the cause, though the probability is that Covey was ashamed to have it known that he had been mastered by a boy of sixteen. He enjoyed the unbounded and very valuable reputation of being a first-rate overseer and negro-breaker, and by means of this reputation he was able to procure his hands at very trifling compensation and with very great ease. His interest and his pride would mutually suggest the wisdom of passing the matter by in silence. The story that he had undertaken to whip a lad and had been resisted, would of itself be damaging to him in the estimation of slaveholders.

It is perhaps not altogether creditable to my natural temper that after this conflict with Mr. Covey I did, at times, purposely aim to provoke him to an attack, by refusing to keep with the other hands in the field ; but I could never bully him to another battle. I was determined on doing him serious damage if he ever again attempted to lay violent hands on me.

> "Hereditary bondmen, know ye not
> Who would be free, themselves must strike the blow ?"

Chapter XVIII.

NEW RELATIONS AND DUTIES.

Change of masters—Benefits derived by change—Fame of the fight with Covey—Reckless unconcern—Author's abhorrence of slavery —Ability to read a cause of prejudice—The holidays—How spent— Sharp hit at slavery—Effects of holidays—Difference between Covey and Freeland—An irreligious master preferred to a religious one—Hard life at Covey's useful to the author—Improved condition does not bring contentment—Congenial society at Freeland's—Author's Sabbath -school—Secrecy necessary—Affectionate relations of tutor and pupils—Confidence and friendship among slaves—Slavery the inviter of vengeance.

M Y term of service with Edward Covey expired on Christmas day, 1834. I gladly-enough left him, although he was by this time as gentle as a lamb. My home for the year 1835 was already secured, my next master selected. There was always more or less excitement about the changing of hands, but determined to fight my way, I had become somewhat reckless and cared little into whose hands I fell. The report got abroad that I was hard to whip ; that I was guilty of kicking back, and that, though generally a good-natured negro, I sometimes "got the devil in me." These sayings were rife in Talbot County and distinguished me among my servile brethren. Slaves would sometimes fight with each other, and even die at each other's hands, but there were very few who were not held in awe by a white man. Trained from the cradle up to think and feel that their masters were superiors, and invested with a sort of sacredness, there were few who could rise above the control which that sentiment exercised. I had freed myself from it, and the thing was known. One bad sheep will spoil a whole flock. I was a bad sheep. I hated slavery, slaveholders, and all pertaining to them; and I did not fail to inspire others with the same feeling wherever and whenever opportunity was presented. This made me a marked lad among the slaves, and a suspected one among slaveholders. A knowledge also of my ability to read and write got pretty widely spread, which was very much against me.

The days between Christmas day and New Year's were allowed the slaves as holidays. During these days all regular work was suspended, and there was nothing to do but to keep fires and look after the stock. We regarded this time as our own by the grace of our masters, and we therefore used it or abused it as we pleased. Those who had families at a distance were expected to visit them and spend with them the entire week. The younger slaves or the unmarried ones were expected to see to the animals and attend to incidental duties at home. The holidays were variously spent. The sober, thinking, industrious ones would employ themselves in manufacturing corn-brooms, mats, horse-collars, and baskets, and some of these were very well made. Another class spent their time in hunting opossums, coons, rabbits, and other game. But the majority spent the holidays in sports, ball-playing, wrestling, boxing, running, foot-races, danc-ing, and drinking whisky; and this latter mode was generally most agreeable to their masters. A slave who would work during the holidays was thought by his master undeserving of holidays. There was in this simple act of continued work an accusation against slaves, and a slave could not help thinking that if he made three dollars during the holidays he might make three hundred during the year. Not to be drunk during the holidays was disgraceful.

The fiddling, dancing, and "jubilee" beating was carried on in all directions. This latter performance was strictly southern. It supplied the place of violin or other musical instruments and was played so easily that almost every farm had its " Juba" beater. The performer improvised as he beat the instrument, marking the words as he sang so as to have them fall pat with the movement of his hands. Once in a while among a mass of nonsense and wild frolic, a sharp hit was given to the meanness of slaveholders. Take the following for example:

We raise de wheat,
Dey gib us de corn:
We bake de bread,
Dey gib us de crust;
We sif de meal,
Dey gib us de huss;

We peel de meat,
Dey gib us de skin;
And dat's de way
Dey take us in;
We skim de pot,
Dey gib us de liquor,

And say dat's good enough for nigger.
Walk over! walk over!
Your butter and de fat;
Poor nigger, you can't get over dat! Walk over—

This is not a bad summary of the palpable injustice and fraud of slavery, giving, as it does, to the lazy and idle the comforts which God designed should be given solely to the honest laborer. But to the holidays. Judging from my own observation and experience, I believe those holidays were among the most effective means in the hands of slaveholders of keeping down the spirit of insurrection among the slaves.

To enslave men successfully and safely it is necessary to keep their minds occupied with thoughts and aspirations short of the liberty of which they are deprived. A certain degree of attainable good must be kept before them. These holidays served the purpose of keeping the minds of the slaves occupied with prospective pleasure within the limits of slavery. The young man could go wooing, the married man to see his wife, the father and mother to see their children, the industrious and money-loving could make a few dollars, the great wrestler could win laurels, the young people meet and enjoy each other's society, the drinking man could get plenty of whisky, and the religious man could hold prayer-meetings, preach, pray, and exhort. Before the holidays there were pleasures in prospect; after the holidays they were pleasures of memory, and they served to keep out thoughts and wishes of a more dangerous character. These holidays were also used as conductors or safety-valves, to carry off the explosive elements inseparable from the human mind when reduced to the condition of slavery. But for these the rigors of bondage would have become too severe for endurance, and the slave would have been forced to a dangerous desperation.

Thus they became a part and parcel of the gross wrongs and inhumanity of slavery. Ostensibly they were institutions of benevolence designed to mitigate the rigors of slave-life, but practically they were a fraud instituted by human selfishness, the better to secure the ends of injustice and oppression. Not the slave's happiness but the master's safety, was the end sought. It was not from a generous unconcern for the slave's labor, but from a prudent regard for the slave system. I am strengthened in this opinion from the fact that most slaveholders liked to have their slaves spend the holidays in such manner as to be of no real benefit to them. Everything like rational enjoyment was frowned upon, and only those wild and low sports peculiar to semi-civilized people were encouraged. The license allowed appeared to have no other object than to disgust the slaves with their temporary freedom, and to make them as glad to return to their work as they had been to leave it. I have known slaveholders resort to cunning tricks, with a view of getting their slaves deplorably drunk. The usual plan was to make bets on a slave that he could drink more whisky than any other, and so induce a rivalry among them for the mastery in this degradation. The scenes brought about in this way were often scandalous and loathsome in the extreme. Whole multitudes might be found stretched out in brutal drunkenness, at once helpless and disgusting. Thus, when the slave asked for hours of " virtuous liberty," his cunning master took advantage of his ignorance and cheered him with a dose of vicious and revolting dissipation artfully labeled with the name of " *liberty.* "

We were induced to drink, I among the rest, and when the holidays were over we all staggered up from our filth and wallowing, took a long breath, and went away to our various fields of work, feeling, upon the whole, rather glad to go from that which our masters had artfully deceived us into the belief was freedom, back again to the arms of slavery. It was not what we had taken it to be, nor what it would have been, had it not been abused by us. It was about as well to be a slave to master, as to be a slave to whisky and rum. When the slave was drunk the slaveholder had no fear that he would plan an insurrection, or that he would escape to the

North. It was the sober, thoughtful slave who was dangerous and needed the vigilance of his master to keep him a slave.

On the first of January, 1835, I proceeded from St. Michaels to Mr. William Freeland's—my *new* home. Mr. Freeland lived only three miles from St. Michaels, on an old, worn-out farm, which required much labor to render it anything like a self-supporting establishment.

I found Mr. Freeland a different man from Covey. Though not rich, he was what might have been called a well-bred Southern gentleman. Though a slaveholder and sharing in common with them many of the viceis of his class, he seemed alive to the sentiment of honor, and had also some sense of justice, and some feelings of humanity. He was fretful, impulsive, and passionate, but free from the mean and selfish characteristics which distinguished the creature from which I had happily escaped. Mr. Freeland was open, frank, and imperative. He practiced no concealments and disdained to play the spy. He was, in all these qualities, the opposite of Covey.

My poor weather-beaten bark now reached smoother water and gentler breezes. My stormy life at Covey's had been of service to me. The things that would have seemed very hard had I gone directly to Mr. Freeland's from the home of Master Thomas, were now " trifles light as air." I was still a field-hand, and had come to prefer the severe labor of the field to the enervating duties of a house-servant. I had become large and strong, and had begun to take pride in the fact that I could do as much hard work as some of the older men. There was much rivalry among slaves at times as to which could do the most work, and masters generally sought to promote such rivalry. But some of us were too wise to race with each other very long. Such racing, we had the sagacity to see, was not likely to pay. We had our times for measuring each other's strength, but we knew too much to keep up the competition so long as to produce an extraordinary day's work. We knew that if by extraordinary exertion a large quantity of work was done in one day, and it became known to the master, it might lead him to require the same amount every day. This thought was enough to bring us to a dead halt when ever so much excited for the race.

At Mr. Freeland's my condition was every way improved. I was no longer the scapegoat that I was when at Covey's, where every wrong thing done was saddled upon me, and where other slaves were whipped over my shoulders. Bill Smith was protected by a positive prohibition, made by his rich master (and the command of the *rich* slaveholder was *law* to the poor one). Hughes was favored by his relationship to Covey, and the hands hired temporarily escaped flogging. I was the general pack-horse; but Mr. Freeland held every man individually responsible for his own conduct. Mr. Freeland, like Mr. Covey, gave his hands enough to eat, but, unlike Mr. Covey, he gave them time to take their meals. He worked us hard during the day, but gave us the night for rest. We were seldom in the field after dark in the evening, or before sunrise in the morning. Our implements of husbandry were of the most improved pattern, and much superior to those used at Covey's.

Notwithstanding all the improvement in my relations, notwithstanding the many advantages I had gained by my new home and my new master, I was still restless and discontented. I was about as *difficult* to be pleased by a master as a master is by a slave. The freedom from bodily torture and unceasing labor had given my mind an increased sensibility and imparted to it greater activity. I was not yet exactly in right relations. " Howbeit, that was not first which is spiritual, but that which is natural, and afterward that which is spiritual." When entombed at Covey's and shrouded in darkness and physical wretchedness, temporal well-being was the grand desideratum ; but, temporal wants supplied, the spirit put in its claims. Beat and cuff the slave, keep him hungry and spiritless, and he will follow the chain of his master like a dog; but feed and clothe him well, work him moderately and surround him with physical comfort, and dreams of freedom will intrude. Give him a *bad* master and he aspires to a good master ; give him a good master, and he wishes to become his own master. Such is human nature. You may hurl a man so low beneath the level of his kind,that he loses all just ideas of his natural position, but elevate him a little, and the clear conception of rights rises to life and power, and leads him onward. Thus elevated a little at Freeland's, the dreams called into being by that good man, Father Lawson, when in Baltimore, began to visit me again. Shoots from the tree of liberty began to put forth buds, and dim hopes of the future began to dawn.

I found myself in congenial society. There were Henry Harris, John Harris, Handy Caldwell, and Sandy Jenkins (this last, of the root-preventive memory).

Henry and John Harris were brothers, and belonged to Mr. Freeland. They were both remarkably bright and intelligent, though neither of them could read. Now for mischief ! I began to address my companions on the subject of education and the advantages of intelligence over ignorance, and, as far as I dared, I tried to show the agency of ignorance in keeping men in slavery. Webster's spelling-book and the Columbian Orator were looked into again. As summer came on and the long Sabbath days stretched themselves over our idleness, I became uneasy and wanted a Sabbath-school in which to exercise my gifts and to impart to my brother-slaves the little knowledge I possessed. A house was hardly necessary in the summer time ; I could hold my school under the shade of an old oak tree as well as any where else. The thing was to get the scholars, and to have them thoroughly imbued with the idea to learn. Two such boys were quickly found in Henry and John, and from them the contagion spread. I was not long in bringing around me twenty or thirty young men, who enrolled themselves gladly in my Sabbath-school, and were willing to meet me regularly under the trees or elsewhere, for the purpose of learning to read. It was surprising with what ease they provided themselves with spelling-books. These were mostly the cast-off books of their young masters or mistresses. I taught at first on our own farm. All were impressed with the necessity of keeping the matter as private as possible, for the fate of the St. Michaels attempt was still fresh in the minds of all. Our pious masters at St. Michaels must not know that a few of their dusky brothers were learning to read the Word of God, lest they should come down upon us with the lash and chain. We might have met to drink whisky, to wrestle, fight, and to do other unseemly things, with no fear of interruption from the saints or the sinners of St. Michaels. But to meet for the purpose of improving the mind and heart, by learning to read the sacred scriptures, was a nuisance to be instantly stopped. The slave holders there, like slaveholders elsewhere, preferred to see the slaves engaged in degrading sports, rather than acting like moral and accountable beings. Had any one, at that time, asked a religious white man in St. Michaels, the names of three men in that town whose lives were most after the pattern of our Lord and Master Jesus Christ, the reply would have been : Garrison West, class-leader, Wright Fairbanks and Thomas Auld, both also class-leaders; and yet these men, armed with mob-like missiles, ferociously rushed in upon my Sabbath-school and forbade our meeting again on pain of having our backs subjected to the bloody lash. This same Garrison West was my class-leader, and I had thought him a Christian until he took part in breaking up my school. He led me no more after that.

The plea for this outrage was then, as it is always, the tyrant's plea of necessity. If the slaves learned to read they would learn something more and something worse. The peace of slavery would be disturbed. Slave rule would be endangered. I do not dispute the soundness of the reasoning. If slavery were right, Sabbath-schools for teaching slaves to read were wrong, and ought to have been put down. These Christian class-leaders were, to this extent, consistent. They had settled the question that slavery was right, and by that standard they determined that Sabbath-schools were wrong. To be sure they were Protestants and held to the great Protestant right of every man to "search the Scriptures" for himself; but then, to all general rules there are exceptions. How convenient! What crimes may not be committed under such ruling ! But my dear class-leading Methodist brethren did not condescend to give me a reason for breaking up the school at St. Michaels. They had determined its destruction, and that was enough.

After getting the school nicely started a second time, holding it in the woods behind the barn, and in the shade of trees, I succeeded in inducing a free colored man who lived several miles from our house to permit me to hold my school in a room at his house. He incurred much peril in doing so, for the assemblage was an unlawful one. I had at one time more than forty pupils, all of the right sort, and many of them succeeded in learning to read. I have had various employments during my life, but to none do I look back with more satisfaction than to this one. An attachment, deep and permanent, sprang up between me and my persecuted pupils, which made my parting from them intensely painful.

Besides my Sunday-school, I devoted three evenings a week to my other fellow slaves during the winter. Those dear souls who came to my Sabbath-school came not because it was popular or reputable to do so, for they came with a liability of having forty stripes laid on their naked backs. In this Christian country men and women were obliged to hide in barns and woods and trees from professing Christians, in order to learn to read the *Holy Bible.* Their minds had been cramped and starved by their cruel masters. The light of education had been completely excluded and their hard earnings had been taken to educate their master's children. I felt a delight in circumventing the tyrants and in blessing the victims of their curses.

To outward seeming the year at Mr. Freeland's passed off very smoothly. Not a blow was given me during the whole year. To the credit of Mr. Freeland, irreligious though he was, it must be stated that he was the best master I ever had until I became my own master and assumed for myself, as I had a right to do, the responsibility of my own existence and the exercise of my own powers.

For much of the happiness, or absence of misery, with which I passed this year, I am indebted to the genial temper and ardent friendship of my brother slaves. They were every one of them manly, generous and brave. Yes, I say they were brave, and I will add, fine-looking. It is seldom the lot of any one to have truer and better friends than were the slaves on this farm. It was not uncommon to charge slaves with great treachery toward each other, but I must say I never loved, esteemed, or confided in men more than I did in these. They were as true as steel, and no band of brothers could be more loving. There were no mean advantages taken of each other, no tattling, no giving each other bad names to Mr. Freeland, and no elevating one at the expense of the other. We never undertook anything of any importance which was likely to affect each other, without mutual consultation. We were generally a unit, and moved together. Thoughts and sentiments were exchanged between us which might well have been considered incendiary had they been known by our masters. The slaveholder, were he kind or cruel, was a slaveholder still, the every-hour violator of the just and inalienable rights of man, and he was therefore every hour silently but surely whetting the knife of vengeance for his own throat. He never lisped a syllable in commendation of the fathers of this republic without inviting the sword, and asserting the right of rebellion for his own slaves.

Chapter XIX.

THE RUNAWAY PLOT.

New Year's thoughts and meditations—Again hired by Freeland— Kindness no compensation for slavery— Incipient steps toward escape—Considerations leading thereto—Hostility to slavery— Solemn vow taken—Plan divulged to slaves—Columbian Orator again—Scheme gains favor—Danger of discovery—Skill of slaveholders— Suspicion and coercion—Hymns with double meaning— Consultation —Pass-word—Hope and fear—Ignorance of geography —Imaginary difficulties—Patrick Henry—Sandy a dreamer—Route to the north mapped out—Objections— Frauds—Passes—Anxieties —Fear of failure—Strange presentiment—Coincidence—Betrayal— Arrests— Resistance—Mrs. Freeland —Prison—Brutal jests—Passes eaten—Denial—Sand}'—Dragged behind horses—Slave-traders—Alone in prison—Sent to Baltimore.

I am now at the beginning of the year 1836. At the opening year the mind naturally occupies itself with the mysteries of life in all its phases—the ideal, the real, and the actual. Sober people then look both ways, surveying the errors of the past and providing against the possible errors of the future. I, too, was thus exercised. I had little pleasure in retrospect, and the future prospect was not brilliant. " Notwithstanding," thought I, " the many resolutions and prayers I have made in behalf of freedom, I am, this first day of the year 1836, still a slave, still wandering in the depths of a miserable bondage. My faculties and powers of body and soul are not my own, but are the property of a fellow-mortal in no sense superior to me, except that he has the physical power to compel me to be owned and controlled by him. By the combined physical force of the community I am his slave—a slave for life." With thoughts like these I was chafed and perplexed, and they rendered me gloomy and disconsolate. The anguish of my mind cannot be written.

At the close of the year, Mr. Freeland renewed the purchase of my services of Mr. Auld for the coming year. His promptness in doing so would have been flattering to my vanity had I been ambitious to win the reputation of being a valuable slave. Even as it was, 1 felt a slight degree of complacency at the circumstance. It showed him to be as well pleased with me as a slave as I was with him as a master. But the kindness of the slave-master only gilded the chain. It detracted nothing from its weight or strength. The thought that men are made for other and better uses than slavery, throve best under the gentle treatment of a kind master. Its grim visage could assume no smiles able to fascinate the partially enlightened slave into a forgetfulness of his bondage, or of the desirableness of liberty.

I was not through the first month of my second year with the kind and gentlemanly Mr. Freeland before I was earnestly considering and devising plans for gaining that freedom which, when I was but a mere child, I had ascertained to be the natural and inborn right of every member of the human family. The desire for this freedom had been benumbed while I was under the brutalizing dominion of Covey, and it had been postponed and rendered inoperative by my truly pleasant Sunday-school engagements with my friends during the year at Mr. Freehand's. It had, however, never entirely subsided. I hated slavery *always*, and my desire for freedom needed only a favorable breeze to fan it to a blaze at any moment. The thought of being only a creature of the *present* and the *past* troubled me, and I longed to have a *future*—a future with hope in it. To be shut up entirely to the past and present is to the soul whose life and happiness is unceasing progress—what the prison is to the body—a blight and a mildew, a hell of horrors. The dawning of this, another year, awakened me from my temporary slumber, and roused into life my latent but long-cherished aspirations for freedom. I became not only ashamed to be contented in slavery, but ashamed to *seem* to be contented, and in my present favorable condition under the mild rule of Mr. Freeland, I am not sure that some kind reader will not condemn me for being over-ambitious, and greatly wanting in humility, when I say the truth, that I now drove from me all thoughts of making the best of my lot, and welcomed only such thoughts as led me away from the house of bondage. The intensity of my desire to be free, quickened by my present favorable circumstances, brought me to the determination to *act* as well as to think and speak.

Accordingly, at the beginning of this year 1836,I took upon me a solemn vow, that the year which had just now dawned upon me should not close without witnessing an earnest attempt, on my part, to gain my liberty. This vow only bound me to make good my own individual escape, but my friendship for my brother-slaves was so affectionate and confiding that I felt it my duty, as well as my pleasure, to give them an opportunity to share in my determination. Toward Henry and John Harris I felt a friendship as strong as one man can feel for another, for I could have died with and for them. To them, therefore, with suitable caution, I began to disclose my sentiments and plans, sounding them the while on the subject of running away, provided a good chance should offer. I need not say that I did my *very best* to imbue the minds of my dear friends with my own views and feelings. Thoroughly awakened now, and with a definite vow upon me, all my little reading which had any bearing on the subject of human rights was rendered available in my communications with my friends. That gem of a book, the Columbian Orator, with its eloquent orations and spicy dialogues denouncing oppression and slavery—telling what had been dared, done, and suffered by men, to obtain the inestimable boon of liberty,—was still fresh in my memory, and its nobly expressed sentiments whirled into the ranks of my speech with the aptitude of well-trained soldiers going through the drill. I here began my public speaking. I canvassed with Henry and John the subject of slavery and dashed against it the condemning brand of God's eternal justice. My fellow-servants were neither indifferent, dull nor inapt. Our feelings were more alike than our opinions. All, however, were ready to act when a feasible plan should be proposed. " Show us how the thing is to be done," said they, " and all else is clear." We were all, except Sandy, quite clear from slave-holding priestcraft. It was in vain that we had been taught from the pulpit at St. Michaels the duty of obe- dience to our masters ; to recognize God as the author of our enslavement; to regard running away as an offense, alike against God and man ; to deem our enslavement a merciful and beneficial arrangement; to esteem our condition in this country a paradise to that from which we had been snatched in Africa ; to consider our hard hands and dark color as God's displeasure, and as pointing us out as the proper subjects of slavery ; that the relation of master and slave was one of reciprocal benefits and that our work was not more serviceable to our masters than our master's thinking was to us. I say it was in vain that the pulpit of St. Michaels had constantly inculcated these plausible doctrines. Nature laughed them to scorn. For my part, I had become altogether too big for my chains. Father Lawson's solemn words of what I ought to be, and what I might be in the providence of God, had not fallen dead on my soul. I was fast verging toward manhood, and the prophesies of my childhood were still unfulfilled. The thought that year after year had passed away, and that my best resolutions to run away had failed and faded and that I was still a slave, with chances for gaining my freedom diminished and still diminishing—was not a matter to be slept over easily. But here came a trouble. Such thoughts and purposes as I now cherished could not agitate the mind long without making themselves manifest to scrutinizing and unfriendly observers. 1 had reason to fear that my sable face might prove altogether too transparent for the safe concealment of my hazardous enterprise. Plans of great moment have leaked through stone walls, and revealed their projectors. But here was no stone wall to hide. my purpose. I would have given my poor tell-tale face for the immovable countenance of an Indian, for it was far from proof against the daily searching glances of those whom I met.

It was the interest and business of slaveholders to study human nature, and the slave nature in particular, with a view to practical results ; and many of them attained astonishing proficiency in this direction. They had to deal not with earth, wood, and stone, but with *men ;* and by every regard they had for their own safety and prosperity they had need to know the material on which they were to work. So much intellect as that surrounding them, required watching. Their safety depended on their vigilance. Conscious of the injustice and wrong they were every hour perpetrating and knowing what they themselves would do were they the victims of such wrongs, they were constantly looking out for the first signs of the dread retribution. They watched, therefore, with skilled and practiced eyes, and learned to read, with great accuracy, the state of mind and heart of the slave, through his sable face. Unusual sobriety, apparent abstraction, sullenness, and indifference,—indeed, any mood out of the common way,—afforded ground for suspicion and inquiry. Relying upon their superior position and wisdom, they would often hector slaves into a confession by affecting to know the truth of their accusations. "You" have got the devil in you, and we'll whip him out of you," they would say. I have often been put thus to the torture on bare suspicion. This system had its disadvantages as well as its opposite— the slave being sometimes whipped into the confession of offenses which he never committed. It will be seen that the good- old rule, "A man is to be held innocent until proved to be guilty," did not hold good on the slave plantation. Suspicion and torture were there the approved methods of getting at the truth. It was necessary, therefore, for me to keep a watch over my deportment, lest the enemy should get the better of me. But with all our caution and studied reserve, I am not sure that Mr. Freeland did not suspect that all was not right with us. It *did* seem that he watched us more narrowly after the plan of escape had been conceived and discussed amongst us. Men seldom see themselves as others see them; and while to ourselves everything connected with our contemplated escape appeared concealed, Mr. Freeland may, with the peculiar prescience of a slave holder, have mastered the huge thought which was disturbing our peace. As I now look back, I am the more inclined to think that he suspected us, because, prudent as we were, I can see that we did many silly things well calculated to awaken suspicion. We were at times remarkably buoyant, singing hymns, and making joyous exclamations, almost as triumphant in their tone as if we had reached a land of freedom and safety. A keen observer might have detected in our repeated singing of

"O Canaan, sweet Canaan,
I am bound for the land of Canaan,"

something more than a hope of reaching heaven. We meant to reach the *North,* and the North was our Canaan.

"I thought I heard them say
There were lions in the way ;
I don't expect to stay
Much longer here.
Run to Jesus, shun the danger.
I don't expect to stay
Much longer here,"

was a favorite air, and had a double meaning. On the lips of some it meant the expectation of a speedy summons to a world of spirits; but on the lips of our company it simply meant a speedy pilgrimage to a free State, and deliverance from all the evils and dangers of slavery. I had succeeded in winning to my scheme a company of live young men, the very flower of the neighborhood, each one of whom would have commanded one thousand dollars in the home market. At New Orleans they would have brought fifteen hundred dollars apiece, and perhaps more. Their names were as follows: Henry Harris, John Harris, Sandy Jenkins, Charles Roberts, and Henry Bailey. I was the youngest but one of the party. I had, however, the advantage of them all in experience, and in a knowledge of letters. This gave me a great influence over them. Perhaps not one of them, left to himself, would have dreamed of escape as a possible thing. They all wanted to be free, but the serious thought of running away had not entered into their minds until I won them to the undertaking.

They were all tolerably well off— for slaves—and had dim hopes of being set free some day by their masters. If any one is to blame for disturbing the quiet of the slaves and slave-masters of the neighborhood of St. Michaels, I AM THE MAN. I claim to be the instigator of the high crime (as the slaveholders regarded it), and I kept life in it till life could be kept in it no longer.

Pending the time of our contemplated departure out of our Egypt, we met often by night, and on every Sunday. At these meetings we talked the matter over, told our hopes and fears, and the difficulties discovered or imagined; and, like men of sense, counted the cost of the enterprise to which we were committing ourselves. These meetings must have resembled, on a small scale, the meetings of the revolutionary conspirators in their primary condition. We were plotting against our (so-called) lawful rulers, with this difference— we sought our own good, and not the harm of our enemies. We did not seek to overthrow them, but to escape from them. As for Mr. Freeland, we all liked him, and would gladly have remained with him *as free men. Liberty* was our aim, and we had now come to think that we had a right to it against every obstacle, even against the lives of our enslavers.

We had several words, expressive of things important to us, which we understood, but which, even if distinctly heard by an outsider, would have conveyed no certain meaning. I hated this secrecy, but where slavery was powerful, and liberty weak, the latter was driven to concealment or destruction.

The prospect was not always bright. At times we were almost tempted to abandon the enterprise, and to try to get back, to that comparative peace of mind which even a man under the gallows might feel when all hope of escape had vanished. We were, at times, confident, bold and determined, and again, doubting, timid and wavering ; whistling, as did the boy in the grave-yard to keep away the spirits.

To look at the map and observe the proximity of Eastern shore, Maryland, to Delaware and Pennsylvania, it may seem to the reader quite absurd to regard the proposed escape as a formidable undertaking. But to *understand,* some one has said, a man must *stand under.* The real distance was great enough, but the imagined distance was, to our ignorance, much greater. Slaveholders sought to impress their slaves with a belief in the boundlessness of slave territory, and of their own limitless power. Our notions of the geography of the country were very vague and indistinct. The distance, however, was not the chief trouble, for the nearer were the lines of a slave state to the borders of a free state the greater was the trouble. Hired kidnappers infested the borders. Then, too, we knew that merely reaching a free state did not free us, that wherever caught we could be returned to slavery. We knew of no spot this side the ocean where we could be safe. We had heard of Canada, then the only real Canaan of the American bondman, simply as a country to which the wild goose and the swan repaired at the end of winter to escape the heat of summer, but not as the home of man. I knew something of theology, but nothing of geography. I really did not know that there was a State of New York, or a State of Massachusetts. I had heard of Pennsylvania, Delaware, and New Jersey, and all the Southern States, but was utterly ignorant of the free States. New York City was our northern limit, and to go there and to be forever harassed with the lia- bility of being hunted down and returned to slavery, with the certainty of being treated ten times worse than ever before, was a prospect which might well cause some hesitation. The case sometimes, to our excited visions, stood thus: At every gate through which we had to pass we saw a watchman; at every ferry a guard; on every bridge a sentinel, and in every wood a patrol or slave-hunter. We were hemmed in on every side. The good to be sought and the evil to be shunned were flung in the balance and weighed against each other. On the one hand stood slavery, a stern reality glaring frightfully upon us, with the blood of millions in its polluted skirts, terrible to behold, greedily devouring our hard earnings and feeding upon our flesh. This was the evil from which to escape. On the other hand, far away, back in the hazy distance where all forms seemed but shadows under the flickering light of the north star, behind some craggy hill or snow-capped mountain, stood a doubtful freedom, half frozen, and beckoning us to her icy domain. This was the good to be sought. The inequality was as great as that between certainty and uncertainty. This in itself was enough to stagger us; but when we came to survey the untrodden road and conjecture the many possible difficulties, we were appalled, and at times, as I have said, were upon the point of giving over the struggle altogether. The reader can have little idea of the phantoms which would flit, in such circumstances, before the uneducated mind of the slave. Upon either side we saw grim death, assuming a variety of horrid shapes. Now it was starvation, causing us, in a strange and friendless land, to eat our own flesh. Now we were contending with the waves and were drowned. Now we were hunted by dogs and overtaken, and torn to pieces by their merciless fangs. We were stung by scorpions, chased by wild beasts, bitten by snakes, and, worst of all, after having succeeded in swimming rivers, encountering wild beasts, sleeping in the woods, and suffering hunger, cold, heat and nakedness, were overtaken by hired kidnappers, who, in the name of law and for the thrice-cursed reward, would, perchance, fire upon us, kill some, wound others and capture all. This dark picture, drawn by ignorance and fear, at times greatly shook our determination, and not unfrequently caused us to

> " Rather bear the ills we had,
> Than flee to others which we knew not of."

I am not disposed to magnify this circumstance in my experience, and yet I think that, to the reader, I shall seem to be so disposed. But no man can tell the intense agony which was felt by the slave when wavering on the point of making his escape. All that he has is at stake, and even that which he has not is at stake also. The life which he has may be lost and the liberty which he seeks may not be gained.

Patrick Henry, to a listening senate which was thrilled by his magic eloquence and ready to stand by him in his boldest flights, could say, " Give me liberty or give me death ;" and this saying was a sublime one, even for a freeman; but incomparably more sublime is the same sentiment when *practically* asserted by men accustomed to the lash and chain, men whose sensibilities must have become more or less deadened by their bondage. With us it was a doubtful liberty, at best, that we sought, and a certain lingering death in the rice-swamps and sugar-fields if we failed. Life is not lightly regarded by men of sane minds. It is precious both to the pauper and to the prince, to the slave and to his master; and yet I believe there was not one among us who would not rather have been shot down than pass away life in hopeless bondage.

In the progress of our preparations Sandy (the root man) became troubled. He began to have distressing dreams. One of these, which happened on a Friday night, was to him of great significance, and I am quite ready to confess that I myself felt somewhat damped by it. He said: " I dreamed last night that I was roused from sleep by strange noises, like the noises of a swarm of angry birds that caused as they passed, a roar which fell upon my ear like a coming gale over the tops of the trees. Looking up to see what it could mean, I saw you, Frederick, in the claws of a huge bird, surrounded by a large number of birds of all colors and sizes. These were all pecking at you, while you, with your arms, seemed to be trying to protect your eyes. Passing over me, the birds flew in a southwesterly direction, and I watched them until they were clean out of sight. Now I saw this as plainly as I now see you; and furder, honey, watch do Friday night dream; dere is sumpon in it shose you born ; dere is indeed, honey." I did not like the dream, but I showed no concern, attributing it to the general excitement and perturbation consequent upon our contemplated plan to escape. I could not, however, at once shake off its effect. I felt that it boded no good. Sandy was unusually emphatic and oracular and his manner had much to do with the impression made upon me.

The plan for our escape, which I recommended and to which my comrades consented, was to take a large canoe owned by Mr. Hamilton, and on the Saturday night previous to the Easter holidays launch out into the Chesapeake bay and paddle with all our might for its head, a distance of seventy miles. On reaching this point we were to turn the canoe adrift and bend' our steps toward the north-star till we reached a free state.

There were several objections to this plan. In rough weather the waters of the Chesapeake are much agitated, and there would be danger, in a canoe, of being swamped by the waves. Another objection was that the canoe would soon be missed, the absent slaves would at once be suspected of having taken it, and we should be pursued by some of the fast-sailing craft out of St. Michaels. Then again, if we reached the head of the bay and turned the canoe adrift, she might prove a guide to our track and bring the hunters after us.

These and other objections were set aside by the stronger ones, which could be urged against every other plan that could then be suggested. On the water we had a chance of being regarded as fishermen, in the service of a master. On the other hand, by taking the land route, through the counties adjoining Delaware, we should be subjected to all manner of interruptions, and many disagreeable questions, which might give us serious trouble. Any white man, if he pleased, was authorized to stop a man of color on any road, and examine and arrest him. By this arrangement many abuses (considered such even by slaveholders) occurred. Cases have been known where freemen, being called upon by a pack of ruffians to show their free papers, have presented them, when the ruffians have torn them up, seized the victim and sold him to a life of endless bondage.

The week before our intended start, I wrote a pass for each of our party, giving him permission to visit Baltimore during the Easter holidays. The pass ran after this manner :

" This is to certify that I, the undersigned, have given the bearer, my servant John, full liberty to go to Baltimore to spend the Easter holidays. W. H.
NEAR ST. MICHAELS, Talbot Co., Md."

Although we were not going to Baltimore, and were intending to land east of North Point, in the direction I had seen the Philadelphia steamers go, these passes might be useful to us in the lower part of the bay, while steering towards Baltimore. These were not, however, to be shown by us until all our answers had failed to satisfy the inquirer. We were all fully alive to the importance of being calm and self-possessed when accosted, if accosted we should be ; and we more than once rehearsed to each other how we should behave in the hour of trial.

Those were long, tedious days and nights. The suspense was painful in the extreme. To balance probabilities, where life and liberty, hang on the result, requires steady nerves. I panted for action, and was glad when the day, at the close of which we were to start, dawned upon us. Sleeping, the night before, was out of the question. I probably felt more deeply than any of my companions, because I was the instigator of the movement. The responsibility of the whole enterprise rested upon my shoulders. The glory of success and the shame and confusion of failure, could not be matters of indifference to me. Our food was prepared, our clothes were packed ; we were already to go, and impatient for Saturday morning—considering that the last of our bondage.

I cannot describe the tempest and tumult of my brain that morning. The reader will please bear in mind that in a slave State an unsuccessful runaway was not only subjected to cruel torture, and sold away to the far South, but he was frequently execrated by the other slaves. He was charged with making the condition of the other slaves intolerable by laying them all under the suspicion of their masters— subjecting them to greater vigilance, and imposing greater limitations on their privileges. I dreaded murmurs from this quarter. It was difficult, too, for a slave-master to believe that slaves escaping had not been aided in their flight by some one of their fellow-slaves. When, therefore, a slave was missing, every slave on the place was closely examined as to his knowledge of the undertaking.

Our anxiety grew more and more intense, as the time of our intended departure drew nigh. It was truly felt to be a matter of life and death with us, and we fully intended to fight, as well as run, if necessity should occur for that-extremity.

But the trial-hour had not yet come. It was easy to resolve, but not so easy to act. I expected there might be some drawing back at the last; it was natural there should be; therefore, during the intervening time, I lost no opportunity to explain away difficulties, remove doubts, dispel fears, and inspire all with firmness. It was too late to look back, and now was the time to go forward. I appealed to the pride of my comrades by telling them that if, after having solemnly promised to go, as they had done, they now failed to make the attempt, they would in effect brand themselves with cowardice, and might well sit down, fold their arms, and acknowledge themselves fit only to be slaves. This detestable character all were unwilling to assume. Every man except Sandy (he, much to our regret, withdrew) stood firm, and at our last meeting we pledged ourselves afresh, and in the most solemn manner, that at the time appointed we would certainly start on our long journey for a free country. This meeting was in the middle of the week, at the end of which we were to start.

Early on the appointed morning we went as usual to the field, but with hearts that beat quickly and anxiously. Any one intimately acquainted with us might have seen that all was not well with us, and that some monster lingered in our thoughts. Our work that morning was the same that it had been for several days past—drawing out and spreading manure. While thus engaged, I had a sudden presentiment, which flashed upon me like lightning in a dark night, revealing to the lonely traveler the gulf before and the enemy behind. I instantly turned to Sandy Jenkins, who was near me, and said: "Sandy,we are betrayed .'—something has just told me so." I felt as sure of it as if the officers were in sight. Sandy said: "Man, dat is strange ; but I feel just as you do." If my mother —then long in her grave—had appeared before me and told me that we were betrayed, I could not at that moment have felt more certain of the fact.

In a few minutes after this, the long, low, and distant notes of the horn summoned us from the field to break fast. I felt as one may be supposed to feel before being led forth to be executed for some great offense. I wanted no breakfast, but for form's sake I went with the other slaves toward the house. My feelings were not disturbed as to the right of running away ; on that point I had no misgiving whatever, but from a sense of the consequences of failure.

In thirty minutes after that vivid impression came the apprehended crash. On reaching the house, and glancing my eye toward the lane gate, the worst was at once made known. The lane gate to Mr. Freeland's house was nearly half a mile from the door, and much shaded by the heavy wood which bordered the main road. I was, however, able to descry four white men and two colored men approaching. The white men were on horseback, and the colored men were walking behind, and seemed to be tied. "It is indeed all over with us; we are surely betrayed" I thought to myself. I became composed, or at least comparatively so, and calmly awaited the result. I watched the ill-omened company entering the gate. Successful flight was impossible, and I made up my mind to stand and meet the evil, whatever it might be, for I was not altogether without a slight hope that things might turn differently from what I had at first feared. In a few moments in came Mr. William Hamilton, riding very rapidly and evidently much excited. He was in the habit of riding very slowly, and was seldom known to gallop his horse. This time his horse was nearly at full speed, causing the dust to roll thick behind him. Mr. Hamilton, though one of the most resolute men in the whole neighborhood, was, nevertheless, a remarkably mild-spoken man, and even when greatly excited his language was cool and circumspect. He came to the door, and inquired if Mr. Frceland was in. I told him that Mr. Freeland was at the barn. Off the old gentleman rode toward the barn, with unwonted speed. In a few moments Mr. Hamilton and Mr. Freeland came down from the barn to the house, and just as they made their appearance in the front-yard, three men, who proved to be constables, came dashing into the lane on horse-back, as if summoned by a sign requiring quick work. A few seconds brought them into the front-yard, where they hastily dismounted and tied their horses. This done, they joined Mr. Freeland and Mr. Hamilton, who were standing a short distance from the kitchen. A few moments were spent as if in consulting how to proceed, and then the whole party walked up to the kitchen-door. There was now no one in the kitchen but myself and John Harris ; Henry and Sandy were yet in the barn. Mr. Freeland came inside the kitchen-door, and, with an agitated voice, called me by name, and told me to come forward; that there were some gentlemen who wished to see me. I stepped toward them at the door, and asked what they wanted ; when the constables grabbed me, and told me that I had better not resist; that I had been in a scrape, or was said to have been in one; that they were merely going to take me where I could be examined; that they would have me brought before my master at St. Michaels, and if the evidence against me was not proved true I should be acquitted. I was now firmly tied, and completely at the mercy of my captors. Resistance was idle. They were five in number and armed to the teeth. When they had secured me, they turned to John Harris and in a few moments succeeded in tying him as firmly as they had tied me. They next turned toward Henry Harris, who had now returned from the barn. "Cross your hands," said the constable to Henry. "I won't," said Henry, in a voice so firm and clear, and in a manner so determined, as for a moment to arrest all proceedings. "Won't you cross your hands ?" said Tom Graham, the constable. "No, I won't" said Henry, with increasing emphasis. Mr. Hamilton, Mr. Freeland, and the officers now came near to Henry. Two of the constables drew out their shining pistols, and swore, by the name of God, that he should cross his hands or they would shoot him down. Each of these hired ruffians now cocked his pistol, and, with fingers apparently on the triggers, presented his deadly weapon to the breast of the unarmed slave, saying, that if he did not cross his hands, he would " blow his d------d heart out of him." " Shoot me, shoot me," said Henry ; " you can't kill me but once. Shoot, shoot, and be damned ! I won't be tied! " This the brave fellow said in a voice as defiant and heroic in its tone as was the language itself; and at the moment of saying it, with the pistols at his very breast, he quickly raised his arms and dashed them from the puny hands of his assassins, the weapons flying in all directions. Now came the struggle. All hands rushed upon the brave fellow and after beating him for some time succeeded in overpowering and tying him. Henry put me to shame ; he fought, and fought bravely. John and I had made no resistance. The fact is, I never saw much use of fighting where there was no reasonable probability of whipping anybody. Yet there was something almost providential in the resistance made by Henry. But for that resistance every soul of us would have been hurried off to the far South. Just a moment previous to the trouble with Henry, Mr. Hamilton mildly said,—and this gave me the unmistakable clue to the cause of our arrest, —"Perhaps we had now better make a search for those protections, which we understand Frederick has written for himself and the rest." Had these passes been found, they would have been point-blank evidence against us, and would have confirmed all the statements of our betrayer. Thanks to the resistance of Henry, the excitement produced by the scuffle drew all attention in that direction, and I succeeded in flinging my pass, unobserved, into the fire. The confusion attendant on the scuffle, and the apprehension of still further trouble, perhaps, led our captors to forego, for the time, any search for "those protections which Frederick was said to have written for his companions"; so we were not yet convicted of the purpose to run away, and it was evident that there was some doubt on the part of all whether we had been guilty of such purpose.

Just as we were all completely tied, and about ready to start toward St. Michaels, and thence to jail, Mrs. Betsey Freeland (mother to William, who was much attached, after the Southern fashion, to Henry and John, they having been reared "from childhood in her house) came to the kitchen-door with her hands full of biscuits, for we had not had our breakfast that morning, and divided them between Henry and John. This done, the lady made the following parting address to me, pointing her bony finger at me: "You devil! you yellow devil! It was you who put it into the heads of Henry and John to run away. But for you, you long-legged, yellow devil, Henry and John would never have thought of running away." I gave the lady a look which called forth from her a scream of mingled wrath and terror, as she slammed the kitchen-door and went in, leaving me, with the rest, in hands as harsh as her own broken voice.

Could the kind reader have been riding along the main road to or from Easton that morning, his eye would have met a painful sight. He would have seen five young men, guilty of no crime save that of preferring liberty to slavery, drawn along the public highway—firmly bound together, tramping through dust and heat, bare-footed and bare-headed—

fastened to three strong horses, whose riders were armed with pistols and daggers, and on their way to prison like felons, and suffering every possible insult from the crowds of idle, vulgar people who clustered round, and heartlessly made their failure to escape the occasion for all manner of ribaldry and sport. As I looked upon this crowd of vile persons, and saw myself and friends thus assailed and persecuted, I could not help seeing the fulfillment of Sandy's dream. I was in the hands of moral vultures, and held in their sharp talons, and was being hurried away toward Easton, in a southeasterly direction, amid the jeers of new birds of the same feather, through every neighborhood we passed. It seemed to me that everybody was out, and knew the cause of our arrest, and awaited our passing in order to feast their vindictive eyes on our misery.

Some said "I ought to be hanged," and others, "I ought to be burned"; others,I ought to have the "hide" taken off my back; while no one gave us a kind word or sympathizing look, except the poor slaves who were lifting their heavy hoes, and who cautiously glanced at us through the post-and-rail fences, behind which they were at work. Our sufferings that morning can be more easily imagined than described. Our hopes were all blasted at one blow. The cruel injustice, the victorious crime, and the helplessness of innocence, led me to ask in my ignorance and weakness: Where is now the God of justice and mercy ? and why have these wicked men the power thus to trample upon our rights, and to insult our feelings I and yet in the next moment came the consoling thought, "the day of the oppressor will come at last." Of one thing I could be glad: not one of my dear friends upon whom I had brought this great calamity, reproached me, either by word or look, for having led them into it. We were a band of brothers, and never dearer to each other than now. The thought which gave us the most pain was the probable separation which would now take place in case we were sold off to the far South, as We were likely to be. While the constables were looking forward, Henry and I being fastened together, could occasionally exchange a word without being observed by the kidnappers who had us in charge. "What shall I do with my pass?' said Henry. "Eat it with your biscuit," said I; "it won't do to tear it up." We were now near St. Michaels. The direction concerning the passes was passed around, and executed. "Own nothing," said I. "Own nothing" was passed round, enjoined, and assented to. Our confidence in each other was unshaken, and we were quite resolved to succeed or fail together; as much after the calamity which had befallen us as before.

On reaching St. Michaels we underwent a sort of examination at my master's store, and it was evident to my mind that Master Thomas suspected the truthfulness of the evidence upon which they had acted in arresting us, and that he only affected, to some extent, the positiveness with which he asserted our guilt. There was nothing said by any of our company which could, in any manner, prejudice our cause, and there was hope yet that we should be able to return to our homes, if for nothing else, at least to find out the guilty man or woman who betrayed us.

To this end we all denied that we had been guilty of intended flight. Master Thomas said that the evidence he had of our intention to run away was strong enough to hang us in a case of murder. "But," said I, "the cases are not equal; if murder were committed,—the thing is done ! but we have not run away. Where is the evidence against us ? We were quietly at our work." I talked thus with unusual freedom, in order to bring out the evidence against us, for we all wanted, above all things, to know who had betrayed us, that we might have something tangible on which to pour our execrations. From something which dropped, in the course of the talk, it appeared that there was but one witness against us, and that that witness could not be produced. Master Thomas would not tell us who his informant was, but we suspected, and suspected one person only. Several circumstances seemed to point Sandy out as our betrayer. His entire knowledge of our plans, his participation in them, his withdrawal from us, his dream and his simultaneous presentiment that we were betrayed, the taking us and the leaving him, were calculated to turn suspicion toward him, and yet we could not suspect him. We all loved him too well to think it possible that he could have betrayed us. So we rolled the guilt on other shoulders.

We were literally dragged, that morning, behind horses, a distance of fifteen miles, and placed in the Easton jail. We were glad to reach the end of our journey, for our pathway had been full of insult and mortification. Such is the power of public opinion, that it is hard, even for the innocent, to feel the happy consolation of innocence when they fall under the maledictions of this power. How could we regard ourselves as in the right, when all about us denounced us as criminals, and had the power and the disposition to treat us as such.

In jail we were placed under the care of Mr. Joseph Graham, the sheriff of the county. Henry and John and myself were placed in one room, and Henry Bailey and Charles Roberts in another by themselves. This separation was intended to deprive us of the advantage of concert, and to prevent trouble in jail.

Once shut up, a new set of tormentors came upon us. A swarm of imps in human shape—the slave-traders and agents of slave-traders—who gathered in every country town of the State watching for chances to buy human flesh (as buzzards watch for carrion), flocked in upon us to ascertain if our masters had placed us in jail to be sold. Such a set of debased and villainous creatures I never saw before and hope never to see again. I felt as if surrounded by a pack of fiends fresh from perdition. They laughed, leered, and grinned at us, saying, "Ah, boys, we have got you, haven't we ? So you were going to make your escape? Where were you going to?" After taunting us in this way as long as they liked, they one by one subjected us to an examination, with a view to ascertain our value, feeling our arms and legs and shaking us by the shoulders, to see if we were sound and healthy, impudently asking us, " how we would like to have them for masters ?" To such questions we were quite dumb (much to their annoyance). One fellow told me, " if he had me he would cut the devil out of me pretty quick."

These negro-buyers were very offensive to the genteel southern Christian public. They were looked upon in respectable Maryland society as necessary but detestable characters. As a class, they were hardened ruffians, made such by nature and by occupation. Yes, they were the legitimate fruit of slavery, and were second in villainy only to the slaveholders themselves who made such a class possible. They were mere hucksters of the slave produce of Maryland and Virginia—coarse, cruel, and swaggering bullies, whose very breathing was of blasphemy and blood.

Aside from these slave-buyers who infested the prison from time to time, our quarters were much more comfortable than we had any right to expect them to be. Our allowance of food was small and coarse, but our room was the best in the jail—neat and spacious, and with nothing about it necessarily reminding us of being in prison but its heavy locks and bolts and the black iron lattice-work at the windows. We were prisoners of state compared with most slaves who were put into that Easton jail. But the place was not one of contentment. Bolts, bars, and grated windows are not acceptable to freedom-loving people of any color. The suspense, too, was painful. Every step on the stairway was listened to, in the hope that the comer would cast a ray of light on our fate. We would have given the hair of our heads for half a dozen words with one of the waiters in Sol. Lowe's hotel. Such waiters were in the way of hearing, at the table, the probable course of things. We could see them flitting about in their white jackets in front of this hotel, but could speak to none of them.

Soon after the holidays were over, contrary to all our expectations, Messrs. Hamilton and Freeland came up to Eastern; not,to make a bargain with " Georgia traders," nor to send us up to Austin Woldfolk, as was usual in the case of runaway-slaves, but to release, from prison, Charles, Henry Harris, Henry Bailey and John Harris, and this, too, without the infliction of a single blow. I was left alone in prison. The innocent had been taken and the guilty left. My friends were separated from me, and apparently forever. This circumstance caused me more pain than any other incident connected with our capture and imprisonment. Thirty-nine lashes on my naked and bleeding back would have been joyfully borne, in preference to this separation from these, the friends of my youth. And yet I could not but feel that I was the victim of something like justice. Why should these young men, who were led into this scheme by me, suffer as much as the instigator? I felt glad that they were released from prison, and from the dread prospect of a life (or death I should rather say) in the rice-swamps. It is due to the noble Henry to say that he was almost as reluctant to leave the prison with me in it as he had been to be tied and dragged to prison. But he and we all knew that we should, in all the likelihoods of the case, be separated, in the event of being sold; and since we were completely in the hands of our owners they concluded it would be best to go peaceably home.

Not until this last separation, dear reader, had I touched those profounder depths of desolation which it is the lot of slaves often to reach. I was solitary and alone within the walls of a stone prison, left to a fate of lifelong misery. I had hoped and expected much, for months before, but my hopes and expectations were now withered and blasted. The ever-dreaded slave life in Georgia, Louisiana, and Alabama—from which escape was next to impossible—now in my loneliness stared me in the face. The possibility of ever becoming anything but an abject slave, a mere machine in the hands of an owner, had now fled, and it seemed to me it had fled forever. A life of living death, beset with the innumerable horrors of the cotton-field and the sugar-plantation, seemed to be my doom. The fiends who rushed into the prison when we were first put there continued to visit me and ply me with questions and tantalizing remarks. I was insulted, but helpless; keenly alive to the demands of justice and liberty, but with no means of asserting them. To talk to those imps about justice or mercy would have been as absurd as to reason with boars and tigers. Lead and steel were the only arguments that they were capable of appreciating, as the events of the subsequent years have proved.

After remaining in this life of misery and despair about a week, which seemed a month, Master Thomas, very much to my surprise and greatly to my relief, came to the prison and took me out, for the purpose, as he said, of sending me to Alabama with a friend of his, who would emancipate me at the end of eight years. I was glad enough to get out of prison, but I had no faith in the story that his friend would emancipate me. Besides, I had never heard of his having a friend in Alabama, and I took the announcement simply as an easy and comfortable method of shipping me off to the far south. There was a little scandal, too, connected with the idea of one Christian selling another to Georgia traders, while it was deemed every way proper for them to sell to others. I thought this friend in Alabama was an invention to meet this difficulty, for Master Thomas was quite jealous of his religious reputation, however unconcerned he might have been about his real Christian character. In these remarks it is possible I do him injustice. He certainly did not exert his power over me as in the case he might have done, but acted, upon the whole, very generously, considering the nature of my offense. He had the power and the provocation to send me, without reserve, into the very Everglades of Florida, beyond the remotest hope of emancipation; and his refusal to exercise that power must be set down to his credit.

After lingering about St. Michaels a few days, and no friend from Alabama appearing, Master Thomas decided to send me back again to Baltimore, to live with his brother Hugh, with whom he was now at peace. Possibly he became so by his profession of religion at the camp-meeting in the Bay-side. Master Thomas told me that he wished me to go to Baltimore and learn a trade; and that if I behaved myself properly he would emancipate me at twenty-five. Thanks for this one beam of hope in the future ! The promise had but one fault—it seemed too good to be true.

Chapter XX.

APPRENTICESHIP LIFE.

Nothing lost in my attempt to run away—Comrades at home—Reasons for sending me away—Return to Baltimore—Tommy changed —Caulking in Gardiner's shipyard—Desperate fight—Its causes— —Conflict between white and black labor—Outrage—Testimony— Master Hugh—Slavery in Baltimore—My condition improves— —New associations—Slaveholder's right to the slave's wages—How to make a discontented slave.

W ELL, dear reader, I am not, as you have probably inferred, a loser by the general upstir described in the foregoing chapter. The little domestic revolution, notwithstanding the sudden snub it got by the treachery of somebody, did not, after all, end so disastrously as when in the iron cage at Easton I conceived it would. The prospect from that point did look about as dark as any that ever cast its gloom over the vision of the anxious, out-looking human spirit. " All's well that ends well!" My affectionate friends, Henry and John Harris, are still with Mr. Freeland. Charles Roberts and Henry Bailey are safe at their homes. I have not, therefore, anything to regret on their account. Their masters have mercifully forgiven them, probably on the ground suggested in the spirited little speech of Mrs. Freeland, made to me just before leaving for the jail. My friends had nothing to regret, either: for while they were watched more closely, they were doubtless treated more kindly than before, and got new assurances that they should some day be legally emancipated, provided their behavior from that time forward should make them deserving. Not a blow was struck any one of them. As for Master Freeland, good soul, he did not believe we were intending to run away at all. Having given—as he thought—no occasion to his boys to leave him, he could not think it probable that they had entertained a design so grievous. This, however, was not the view taken of the matter by " Mas' Billy," as we used to call the soft-spoken but crafty and resolute Mr. William Hamilton. He had no doubt that the crime had been meditated, and regarding me as the instigator of it, he frankly told Master Thomas that he must remove me from that neighborhood or he would shoot me. He would not have one so dangerous as " Frederick" " tampering with his slaves. William Hamilton was not a man whose threat might be safely disregarded. I have no doubt that, had his warning been disregarded, he would have proved as good as his word. He was furious at the thought of such a piece of high-handed *theft* as we were about to perpetrate—the stealing of our own bodies and souls. The feasibility of the plan, too, could the first steps have been taken, was marvelously plain. Besides, this was a *new* idea, this use of the Bay. Slaves escaping, until now, had taken to the woods ; they had never dreamed of profaning and abusing the waters of the noble Chesapeake by making them the highway from slavery to freedom. Here was a broad road leading to the destruction of slavery, which had hitherto been looked upon as a wall of security by the slaveholders. But Master Billy could not get Mr. Freeland to see matters precisely as he did, nor could he get Master Thomas, excited as he was, to so see them. The latter, I must say it to his credit, showed much humane feeling, and atoned for much that had been harsh, cruel, and unreasonable in his former treatment of me and of others. My " Cousin Tom" told me that while I was in jail Master Thomas was very unhappy, and that the night before his going up to release me he had walked the floor nearly all night, evincing great distress ; that very tempting offers had been made to him by the negro-traders, but he had rejected them all, saying that *money could not tempt him to sell me to the far south.* I can easily believe all this, for he seemed quite reluctant to send me away at all. He told me that he only consented to do so because of the very strong prejudice against me in the neighborhood, and that he feared for my safety if I remained there.

Thus, after three years spent in the country, roughing it in the field, and experiencing all sorts of hardships, I was again permitted to return to Baltimore, the very place of all others, short of a free State, where I most desired to live. The three years spent in the country had made some difference in me, and in the household of Master Hugh. " Little Tommy" was no longer little Tommy, and I was not the slender lad who had left the Eastern Shore just three years before. The loving relations between Master Tommy and myself were broken up. He was no longer dependent on me for protection, but felt himself a *man,* and had other and more suitable associates. In childhood he had considered me scarcely inferior to himself,—certainly quite as good as any other boy with whom he played ; but the time had come when his *friend* must be his slave. So we were cold to each other, and parted. It was a sad thing to me, that, loving each other as we had done, we must now take different roads. To him a thousand avenues were open. Education had made him acquainted with all the treasures of the world and liberty had flung open the gates thereunto ; but I who had attended him seven years; who had watched over him with the care of a big brother, fighting his battles in the street and shielding him from harm to an extent which induced his mother to say,

" Oh, Tommy is always safe when he is with Freddy"—I must be confined to a single condition. He had grown and become a *man:* I, though grown to the stature of manhood, must all my life remain a minor—a mere boy. Thomas Auld, junior, obtained a situation on board the brig Tweed, and went to sea. I have since heard of his death.

There were few persons to whom I was more sincerely attached than to him.

Very soon after I went to Baltimore to live, Master Hugh succeeded in getting me hired to Mr. William Gardiner, an extensive ship-builder on Fell's Point. I was placed there to learn to calk, a trade of which I already had some knowledge, gained while in Mr. Hugh Auld's ship-yard. Gardiner's, however, proved a very unfavorable place for the accomplishment of the desired object. Mr. Gardiner was that season engaged in building two large man-of-war vessels, professedly for the Mexican government. These vessels were to be launched in the month of July of that year, and in failure thereof Mr. Gardiner would forfeit a very considerable sum of money. So, when I entered the ship-yard, all was hurry and driving. There were in the yard about one hundred men; of these, seventy or eighty were regular carpenters —privileged men. There was no time for a raw hand to learn anything. Every man had to do that which he knew how to do, and in entering the yard Mr. Gardiner had directed me to do whatever the carpenters told me to do. This was placing me at the beck and call of about seventy-five men. I was to regard all these as my masters. Their word was to be my law. My situation was a trying one. I was called a dozen ways in the space of a single minute. I needed a dozen pairs of hands. Three or four voices would strike my ear at the same moment. It was " Fred, come help me to cant this timber here,"— "Fred, come carry this timber yonder,"—

"Fred, bring that roller here," —" Fred, go get a fresh can of water," "Fred, come help saw off the end of this timber,"— "Fred, go quick and get the crow-bar,"—"Fred, hold on the end of this fall,"—"Fred, go to the blacksmith's shop and get a new punch,"—" Halloo, Fred! run and bring me a cold-chisel,"—" I say, Fred, bear a hand, and get up a fire under the steam-box as quick as lightning,"—" Hullo, nigger! come turn this grindstone,"—"Come, come; move, move! and *bowse* this timber forward,"—" I say, darkey, blast your eyes! why don't you heat up some pitch?"—"Halloo! halloo! halloo! (three voices at the same time)"—"Come here; go there; hold on where you are. D—n you, if you move I'll knock your brains out!" Such, my dear reader, is a glance at the school which was mine during the first eight months of my stay at Gardiner's ship-yard. At the end of eight months Master Hugh refused longer to allow me to remain with Gardiner. The circumstance which led to this refusal was the committing of an outrage upon me, by the white apprentices of the ship-yard. The fight was a desperate one, and I came out of it shockingly mangled. I was cut and bruised in sundry places, and my left eye was nearly knocked out of its socket. The facts which led to this brutal outrage upon me illustrate a phase of slavery which was destined to become an important element in the overthrow of the slave system, and I may therefore state them with some minuteness. That phase was this —the conflict of slavery with the interests of white mechanics and laborers. In the country this conflict was not so apparent; but in cities, such as Baltimore, Rich-mond, New Orleans, Mobile, etc., it was seen pretty clearly. The slaveholders, with a craftiness peculiar to themselves, by encouraging the enmity of the poor laboring white man against the blacks, succeeded in making the said white man almost as much a slave as the black slave himself. The difference between the white slave and the black slave was this: the latter belonged to one slaveholder, while the former belonged to the slaveholders collectively. The white slave had taken from him by indirection what the black slave had taken from him directly and without ceremony. Both were plundered, and by the same plunderers. The slave was robbed by his master of all his earnings, above what was required for his bare - physical necessities, and the white laboring man was robbed by the slave system of the just results of his labor, because he was flung into competition with a class of laborers who worked without wages. The slaveholders blinded them' to this competition by keeping alive their prejudice against the slaves as *men*—not against them as *slaves.* They appealed to their pride, often denouncing emancipation as tending to place the white working man on an equality with negroes, and by this means they suc- ceeded in drawing off the minds of the poor whites from the real fact, that by the rich slave master they were already regarded as but a single remove from equality with the slave. The impression was cunningly made that slavery was the only power that could prevent the laboring white man from falling to the level of the slave's poverty and degradation. To make this enmity deep and broad between the slave and the poor white man, the latter was allowed to abuse and whip the former without hindrance. But, as I have said, this state of affairs pre- vailed *mostly* in the country. In the city of Baltimore there were not unfrequent murmurs that educating slaves to be mechanics might, in the end, give slave-masters power to dispense altogether with the services of the poor white man. But with characteristic dread of offending the slaveholders, these poor white mechanics in Mr. Gardiner's ship-yard, instead of applying the natural, honest remedy for the apprehended evil, and objecting at once to work there by the side of slaves, made a cowardly attack upon the free colored mechanics, saying they were eating the bread which should be eaten by American freemen, and swearing that they, the mechanics, would not work with them. The feeling was *really* against having their labor brought into competition with that of the colored freeman, and aimed to prevent him from serving himself, in the evening of life, with the trade with which he had served his master, during the more vigorous portion of his days. Had they succeeded in driving the black freemen out of the ship-yard, they would have determined also upon the removal of the black slaves. The feeling was, about this time, very bitter toward all colored people in Baltimore (1836), and they—free and slave—suffered all manner of insult and wrong.

Until a very little while before I went there, white and black carpenters worked side by side in the shipyards of Mr. Gardiner, Mr. Duncan, Mr. Walter Price and Mr. Robb. Nobody seemed to see any impropriety in it. Some of the blacks were first-rate workmen and were given jobs requiring the highest skill. All at once, however, the white carpenters swore that they would no longer work on the same stage with negroes. Taking advantage of the heavy contract resting upon Mr. Gardiner to have the vessels for Mexico ready to launch in July, and of the difficulty of getting other hands at that season of the year, they swore that they would not strike another blow for him unless he would discharge his free colored workmen. Now, although this movement did not extend to me *in form,* it did reach me in *fact.* The spirit which it awakened was one of malice and bitterness toward colored people *generally,* and I suffered with the rest, and suffered severely. My fellow-apprentices very soon began to feel it to be degrading to work with me. They began to put on high looks and to talk contemptuously and maliciously of

" the niggers," saying that they would take the " country," and that they " ought to he killed." Encouraged by workmen who, knowing me to be a slave, made no issue with Mr. Gardiner about my being there, these young men did their utmost to make it impossible for me to stay. They seldom called me to do anything without coupling the call with a curse, and Edward North, the biggest in everything, rascality included, ventured to strike me, whereupon I picked him up and threw him into the dock. Whenever any of them struck me I struck back again, regardless of consequences. I could manage any of them *singly,* and so long as I could keep them from combining I got on very well. In the conflict which ended my stay at Mr. Gardiner's I was beset by four of them at once—Ned North, Ned Hayes, Bill Stewart, and Tom Humphreys. Two of them were as large as myself, and they came near killing me, in broad daylight. One came in front, armed with a brick; there was one at each side and one behind, and they closed up all around me. I was struck on all sides; and while I was attending to those in front I received a blow on my head from behind, dealt with a heavy hand-spike. I was completely stunned by the blow, and fell heavily on the ground among the timbers. Taking advantage of my fall they rushed upon me and began to pound me with their fists. With a view of gaining strength, I let them lay on for awhile after I came to myself. They had done me little damage, so far; but finally getting tired of that sport I gave a sudden surge, and despite their weight I rose to my hands and knees. Just as I did this one of their number planted a blow with his boot in my left eye, which for a time seemed to have burst my eye-ball. When they saw my eye completely closed, my face covered with blood, and I staggering under the stunning blows they had given me, they left me. As soon as I gathered strength I picked up the hand-spike and madly enough attempted to pursue them; but here the carpenters interfered and compelled me to give up my pursuit. It was impossible to stand against so many.

Dear reader, you can hardly believe the statement, but it is true and therefore I write it down ; that no fewer than fifty white men stood by and saw this brutal and shameful outrage committed, and not a man of them all interposed a single word of mercy. There were four against one, and that one's face was beaten and battered most horribly, and no one said, "that is enough;" but some cried out, "Kill him! kill him! kill the d—n nigger ! knock his brains out! he struck a white person !" I mention this inhuman outcry to show the character of the men and the spirit of the times at Gardiner's ship-yard ; and, indeed, in Baltimore generally, in 1836. As I look back to this period, I am almost amazed that I was not murdered outright, so murderous was the spirit which prevailed there. On two other occasions while there I came near losing my life. On one of these, I was driving bolts in the hold through the keelson, with Hayes. In its course the bolt bent. Hayes cursed me and said that it was my blow which bent the bolt. I denied this and charged it upon him. In a fit of rage he seized an adze and darted toward me. I met him with a maul and parried his blow, or I should have lost my life.

After the united attack of North, Stewart, Hayes, and Humphreys, finding that the carpenters were as bitter toward me as the apprentices, and that the latter were probably set on by the former, I found my only chance for life was in flight. I succeeded in getting away without an additional blow. To strike a white man was death by lynch law, in Gardiner's ship-yard ; nor was there much of any other law toward the colored people at that time in any other part of Maryland.

After making my escape from the ship-yard I went straight home and related my story to Master Hugh ; and to his credit I say it, that his conduct, though he was not a religious man, was every way more humane than that of his brother Thomas, when I went to him in a somewhat similar plight, from the hands of his " Brother Edward Covey." Master Hugh listened attentively to my narration of the circumstances leading to the ruffianly assault, and gave many evidences of his strong indignation at what was done. He was a rough but manly-hearted fellow, and at this time his best nature showed itself.

The heart of my once kind mistress Sophia was again melted in pity towards me. My puffed-out eye and my scarred and blood-covered face moved the dear lady to tears. She kindly drew a chair by me, and with friendly and consoling words, she took water and washed the blood from my face. No mother's hand could have been more tender than hers. She bound up my head and covered my wounded eye with a lean piece of fresh beef. It was almost compensation for all I suffered, that it occasioned the manifestation once more of the originally characteristic kindness of my mistress. Her affectionate heart was not yet dead, though much hardened by time and circumstances.

As for Master Hugh, he was furious, and gave expression to his feelings in the forms of speech usual in that locality. He poured curses on the whole of the ship-yard company, and swore that he would have satisfaction. His indignation was really strong and healthy; but unfortunately it resulted from the thought that his rights of property, in my person, had not been respected, more than from any sense of the outrage perpetrated upon me *as a man.* I had reason to think this from the fact that he could, himself, beat and mangle when it suited him to do so.

Bent on having satisfaction, as he said, just as soon as I got a little the better of my bruises Master Hugh took me to

Esquire Watson's office on Bond street, Fell's Point, with a view to procuring the arrest of those who had assaulted me. He gave to the magistrate an account of the outrage as I had related it to him, and seemed to expect that a warrant would at once be issued for the arrest of the lawless ruffians. Mr. Watson heard all that he had to say, then coolly inquired, " Mr. Auld, who saw this assault of which you speak ?" " It was done, sir, in the presence of a ship-yard full of hands." " Sir," said Mr. Watson, " I am sorry, but I cannot move in this matter, except upon the oath of white witnesses." " But here's the boy ; look at his head and face," said the excited Master Hugh ; *"they* show *what* has been done." But Watson insisted that he was not authorized to do anything, unless white witnesses of the transaction would come forward and testify to what had taken place. He could issue no warrant, on my word, against white persons, and if I had been killed in the presence of a *thousand blacks,* their testimony combined would have been insufficient to condemn a single murderer. Master Hugh was compelled to say, for once, that this state of things was *too* bad, and he left the office of the magistrate disgusted.

Of course it was impossible to get any white man to testify against my assailants. The carpenters saw what was done ; but the actors were but the agents of their malice, and did only what the carpenters sanctioned. They had cried with one accord, " Kill the nigger ! kill the nigger! " Even those who may have pitied me, if any such were among them, lacked the moral courage to volunteer their evidence. The slightest show of sympathy or justice toward a person of color was denounced as abolitionism; and the name of abolitionist subjected its hearer to frightful liabilities. " D--n abolitionists," and " kill the niggers," were the watch-words of the foul-moutbed ruffians of those days. Nothing was done, and probably would not have been, had I been killed in the affray. The laws and the morals of the Christian city of Baltimore afforded no protection to the sable denizens of that city.

Master Hugh, on finding that he could get no redress for the cruel wrong, withdrew me from the employment of Mr. Gardiner and took me into his own family, Mrs. Auld kindly taking care of me and dressing my wounds until they were healed and I was ready to go to work again.

While I was on the Eastern Shore, Master Hugh had met with reverses which overthrew his business and had given up ship-building in his own yard, on the City Block, and was now acting as foreman of Mr. Walter Price. The best that he could do for me was to take me into Mr. Price's yard, and afford me the facilities there for completing the trade which I began to learn at Gardiner's. Here I rapidly became expert in the use of calkers' tools, and in the course of a single year, I was able to command the highest wages paid to journeymen calkers in Baltimore.

The reader will observe that I was now of some pecuniary value to my master. During the busy season I was bringing six and seven dollars per week. I have sometimes brought him as much as nine dollars a week, for wages were a dollar and a half per day.

After learning to calk, I sought my own employment, made my own contracts, and collected my own earnings — giving Master Hugh no trouble in any part of the transactions to which I was a party.

Here, then, were better days for the Eastern Shore *slave*. I was free from the vexatious assaults of the apprentices at Gardiner's; free from the perils of plantation life and once more in favorable condition to increase my little stock of education, which had been at a dead stand since my removal from Baltimore. I had on the Eastern Shore been only a teacher, when in company with other slaves, but now there were colored persons here who could instruct me. Many of the young calkers could read, write, and cipher. Some of them had high notions about mental improvement, and the free ones on Fell's Point organized what they called the " East Baltimore Mental Improvement Society." To this society, notwithstanding it was intended that only free persons should attach themselves, I was admitted, and was several times assigned a prominent part in its debates. I owe much to the society of these young men. The reader already knows enough of the *ill* effects of good treatment on a slave to anticipate what was now the case in my improved condition. It was not long before I began to show signs of disquiet with slavery, and to look around for means to get out of it by the shortest route. I was living among *freemen,* and was in all respects equal to them by nature and attainments. *Why should I be a slave ?* There was *no* reason why I should be the thrall of any man. Besides, I was now getting, as I have said, a dollar and fifty cents per day. I contracted for it, worked for it, collected it; it was paid to me, and it was *rightfully* my own ; and yet upon every returning Saturday night, this money—my own hard earnings, every cent of it, —was demanded of me and taken from me by Master Hugh. He did not earn it; he had no hand in earning it; why, then should he have it? I owed him nothing. He had given me no schooling, and I had received from him only my food and raiment; and for these,my services were supposed to pay from the first. The right to take my earnings was the right of the robber. He had the power to compel me to give him the fruits of my labor, and this *power* was his only right in the case. I became more and more dissatisfied with this state of things, and in so becoming I only gave proof of the same human nature which every reader of this chapter in my life—slaveholder, or non-slaveholder—is conscious of possessing.

To make a contented slave, you must make a thoughtless one. It is necessary to darken his moral and mental vision, and,as far as possible, to annihilate his power of reason. He must be able to detect no inconsistencies in slavery. The man who takes his earnings must be able to convince him that he has a perfect right to do so. It must not depend upon mere force : the slave must know no higher law than his master's will. The whole relationship must not only demonstrate to his mind its necessity, but its absolute rightfulness. If there be one crevice through which a single drop can fall, it will certainly rust off the slave's chain.

Chapter XXI.

ESCAPE FROM SLAVERY.

Closing incidents in my " Life as a Slave"—Discontent—Suspicions —Master's generosity—Difficulties in the way of escape—Plan to obtain money—Allowed to hire my time—A gleam of hope—Attend camp -meeting—Anger of Master Hugh—The result—Plans of Escape—Day for departure fixed—Harrassing doubts and fears—Pain ful thoughts of separation from friends.

MY condition during the year of my escape (1838) was comparatively a free and easy one, so far, at least, as the wants of the physical man were concerned ; but the reader will bear in mind that my troubles from the beginning had been less physical than mental, and he will thus be prepared to find that slave life was adding nothing to its charms for me as I grew older, and became more and more acquainted with it. The practice of openly robbing me, from week to week, of all my earnings, kept the nature and character of slavery constantly before me. I could be robbed by indirection, but this was too open and barefaced to be endured. I could see no reason why I should, at the end of each week, pour the reward of my honest toil into the purse of my master. My obligation to do this vexed me, and the manner in which Master Hugh received my wages vexed me yet more. Carefully counting the money, and rolling it out dollar by dollar, he would look me in the face, as if he would search my heart as well as my pocket, and reproachfully ask me, " Is that all ?"—implying that I had perhaps kept back part of my wages; or, if not so, the demand was made possibly to make me feel that after all, I was an " unprofitable servant." Draining me of the last cent of my hard earnings, he would, however, occasionally, when I brought home an extra large sum, dole out to me a sixpence or shilling, with a view, perhaps, of kindling my gratitude. But it had the opposite effect. It was an admission of my right to the whole sum. The fact that he gave me any part of my wages, was proof that he suspected I had a right to the whole of them ; and I always felt uncomfortable after having received anything in this way, lest his giving me a few cents might possibly ease his conscience, and make him feel himself to be a pretty honorable robber after all.

Held to a strict account, and kept under a close watch, —the old suspicion of my running away not having been entirely removed,—to accomplish my escape seemed a very difficult thing. The railroad from Baltimore to Philadelphia was under regulations so stringent that even *free* colored travelers were almost excluded. They must have free papers; they must be measured and carefully examined before they could enter the cars, and could go only in the day time, even when so examined. The steamboats were under regulations equally stringent. And still more, and worse than all, all the great turnpikes leading northward were beset with kidnappers; a class of men who watched the newspapers for advertisements for runaway slaves, thus making their living by the accursed reward of slave-hunting.

My discontent grew upon me, and I was on a constant look-out for means to get away. With money I could easily have managed the matter, and from this consideration I hit upon the plan of soliciting the privilege of hiring my time. It was quite common in Baltimore to allow slaves this privilege, and was the practice also in New Orleans. A slave who was considered trustworthy could, by regularly paying his master a definite sum at the end of each week, dispose of his time as he liked. It so happened that I was not in very good odor, and was far from being a trustworthy slave. Nevertheless, I watched my opportunity when Master Thomas came to Baltimore (for I was still his property, Hugh only acting as his agent,) in the spring of 1838, to purchase his spring supply of goods, and applied to him directly for the much-coveted privilege of hiring my time. This request Master Thomas unhesitatingly refused to grant and charged me, with some sternness, with inventing this stratagem to make my escape. He told me I could go *nowhere* but he would catch me; and, in the event of my running away, I might be assured that he should spare no pains in his efforts to recapture me. He recounted, with a good deal of eloquence, the many kind offices he had done me, and exhorted me to be contented and obedient. "Lay out no plans for the future," said he. "If you behave yourself properly, I will take care of you." Kind and considerate as this offer was, it failed to soothe me into repose. In spite of all Master Thomas had said and in spite of my own efforts to the contrary, the injustice and wickedness of slavery were always uppermost in my thoughts and strengthening my purpose to make my escape at the earliest moment possible.

About two months after applying to Master Thomas for the privilege of hiring my time, I applied to Master Hugh for the same liberty, supposing him to be unacquainted with the fact that I had made a similar application to Master Thomas and had been refused. My boldness in making this request fairly astounded him at first. He gazed at me in amazement. But I had many good reasons for pressing the matter, and, after listening to them awhile, he did not absolutely refuse but told me that he would think of it. There was hope for me in this. Once master of my own time, I felt sure that I could make, over and above my obligation to him, a dollar or two every week. Some slaves had, in this way, made enough to purchase their freedom. It was a sharp spur to their industry ; and some of the most enterprising colored men in Baltimore hired themselves in that way.

After mature reflection, as I suppose it was, Master Hugh granted me the privilege in question, on the following terms: I was to be allowed all my time; to make all bargains for work, and to collect my own wages ; and in return for this liberty, I was required or obliged to pay him three dollars at the end of each week, and to board and clothe myself, and buy my own calking tools. A failure in any of these particulars would put an end to the privilege. This was a hard bargain. The wear and tear of clothing, the losing and breaking of tools, and the expense of board, made it necessary for me to earn at least six dollars per week to keep even with the world. All who are acquainted with calking know how uncertain and irregular that employment is. It can be done to advantage only in dry weather, for it is useless to put wet oakum into a ship's seam. Rain or shine, however, work or no work, at the end of each week the money must be forthcoming.

Master Hugh seemed, for a time, much pleased with this arrangement; and well he might be, for it was decidedly in his favor. It relieved him of all anxiety concerning me. His money was sure. He had armed my love of liberty with a lash and a driver far more efficient than any I had before known ; for, while by this arrangement, he derived all the benefits of slaveholding without its evils, I endured all the evils of being a slave, and yet suffered all the care and anxiety of a responsible freeman. "Nevertheless," thought I, "it is a valuable privilege—another step in my career toward freedom." It was something even to be permitted to stagger under the disadvantages of liberty, and I was determined to hold on to the newly gained footing by all proper industry. I was ready to work by night as by day, and being in the possession of excellent health, I was not only able to meet my current expenses, but also to lay by a small sum at the end of each week. All went on thus from the month of May till August; then, for reasons which will become apparent as I proceed, my much-valued liberty was wrested from me.

During the week previous to this calamitous event, I had made arrangements with a few young friends to accompany them on Saturday night to a camp-meeeting, to be held about twelve miles from Baltimore. On the evening of our intended start for the camp-ground, something occurred in the ship-yard where I was at work which detained me unusually late, and compelled me either to disappoint my friends, or to neglect carrying my weekly dues to Master Hugh. Knowing that I had the money and could hand it to him on another day, I decided to go to camp-meeting and, on my return, to pay him the three dollars for the past week. Once on the camp-ground, I was induced to remain one day longer than I had intended when I left home. But as soon as I returned I went directly to his home on Fell street to hand him his (my) money. Unhappily the fatal mistake had been made. I found him exceedingly angry. He exhibited all the signs of apprehension and wrath which a slaveholder might be surmised to exhibit on the supposed escape of a favorite slave. " You rascal! I have a great mind to give you a sound whipping. How dare you go out of the city without first asking and obtaining my permission?" "Sir," 1 said, "I hired my time and paid you the price you asked for it. I did not know that it was any part of the bargain that I should ask you when or where I should go." " You did not know, you rascal! You are bound to show yourself here every Saturday night." After reflecting a few moments, he became somewhat cooled down, but, evidently greatly troubled, said: " Now, you scoundrel, you have done for yourself; you shall hire your time no longer. The next thing 1 shall hear of will be your running away. Bring home your tools at once. I'll teach you how to go off in this way."

Thus ended my partial freedom. I could hire my time no longer. I obeyed my master's orders at once. The little taste of liberty which I had had—although as it will be seen, that taste was far from being unalloyed,— by no means enhanced my contentment with slavery. Punished by Master Hugh, it was now my turn to punish him. "Since," thought I, " you *will* make a slave of me, I will await your order in all things." So, instead of going to look for work on Monday morning, as I had formerly done, I remained at home during the entire week, without the performance of a single stroke of work. Saturday night came, and he called upon me as usual for my wages. I, of course, told him I had done no work, and had no wages. Here we were at the point of coming to blows. His wrath had been accumulating during the whole week; for he evidently saw that I was making no effort to get work, but was most aggravatingly awaiting his orders in all things. As I look back to this behavior of mine, I scarcely know what possessed me, thus to trifle with one who had such unlimited power to bless or blast me. Master Hugh raved, and swore he would " get hold of me," but wisely for *him,* and happily for *me,* his wrath employed only those harmless, impalpable missiles which roll from a limber tongue. In my desperation I had fully made up my mind to measure strength with him in case he should attempt to execute his threat. I am glad there was no occasion for this, for resistance to him could not have ended so happily for me as it did in the case of Covey. Master Hugh was not a man to be safely resisted by a slave ; and I freely own that in my conduct toward him, in this instance, there was more folly than wisdom. He closed his reproofs by telling me that hereafter I need give myself no uneasiness about getting work; he " would himself see to getting work for me, and enough of it at that." This threat, I confess, had some terror in it, and on thinking the matter over during the Sunday, I resolved not only to save him the trouble of getting me work, but that on the third day of September I would attempt to make my escape. His refusal to allow me to hire my time therefore hastened the period of my flight. I had three weeks in which to prepare for my journey.

Once resolved, I felt a certain degree of repose, and on Monday morning, instead of waiting for Master Hugh to seek employment for me, I was up by break of day, and off to the ship-yard of Mr. Butler, on the City Block, near the draw-bridge. I was a favorite with Mr. Butler, and, young as I was, I had served as his foreman, on the float-stage, at calking. Of course I easily obtained work, and at the end of the week, which, by the way, was exceedingly fine, I brought Master Hugh nine dollars. The effect of this mark of returning good sense on my part was excellent. He was very much pleased ; he took the money, commended me and told me that I might have done the same thing' the week before. It is a blessed thing that the tyrant may not always know the thoughts and purposes of his victim. Master Hugh little knew my plans. The going to camp-meeting without asking his permission; the insolent answers to his reproaches and the sulky deportment of the week after being deprived of the privilege of hiring my time, had awakened the suspicion that I might be cherishing disloyal purposes. My object, therefore, in working steadily was to remove suspicion ; and in this I succeeded admirably- He probably thought that I was never better satisfied with my condition than at the very time I was planning my escape. The second week passed, and I again carried him my full week's wages—*nine dollars;* and so well pleased was he that he gave me *twenty-five cents*

! and bade me " make good use of it." I told him I would do so, for one of the uses to which I intended to put it was to pay my fare on the " underground railroad."

Things without went on as usual; but I was passing through the same internal excitement and anxiety which I had experienced two years and a half before. The failure in that instance was not calculated to increase my confidence in the success of this, my second attempt; and I knew that a second failure could not leave me where my first did. I must either get to the far North or be sent to the far South. Besides the exercise of mind from this state of facts, I had the painful sensation of being about to separate from a circle of honest and warm hearted friends The thought of such a separation, where the hope of ever meeting again was excluded, and where there could be no correspondence, was very painful. It is my opinion that thousands more would have escaped from slavery but for the strong affection which bound them to their families, relatives, and friends. The daughter was hindered by the love she bore her mother and the father by the love he bore his wife and children, and so on to the end of the chapter. I had no relations in Baltimore, and I saw no probability of ever living in the neighborhood of sisters and brothers ; but the thought of leaving my friends was the strongest obstacle to my running away. The last two days of the week, Friday and Saturday, were spent mostly in collecting my things together for my journey. Having worked four days that week for my master, I handed him six dollars on Saturday night. I seldom spent my Sundays at home, and for fear that something might be discovered in my conduct, I kept up my custom and absented myself all day. On Monday, the third day of September, 1838, in accordance with my resolution, I bade farewell to the city of Baltimore, and to that slavery which had been my abhorrence from childhood.

WHAT TO THE SLAVE IS THE FOURTH OF JULY?

A Speech by Frederick Douglass

MR. President, Friends and Fellow Citizens:

He who could address this audience without a quailing sensation, has stronger nerves than I have. I do not remember ever to have appeared as a speaker before any assembly more shrinkingly, nor with greater distrust of my ability, than I do this day. A feeling has crept over me, quite unfavorable to the exercise of my limited powers of speech. The task before me is one which requires much previous thought and study for its proper performance. I know that apologies of this sort are generally considered flat and unmeaning. I trust, however, that mine will not be so considered. Should I seem at ease, my appearance would much misrepresent me. The little experience I have had in addressing public meetings, in country schoolhouses, avails me nothing on the present occasion.

The papers and placards say, that I am to deliver a 4th [of] July oration. This certainly sounds large, and out of the common way, for it is true that I have often had the privilege to speak in this beautiful hall, and to address many who now honor me with their presence. But neither their familiar faces, nor the perfect gage I think I have of Corinthian Hall, seems to free me from embarrassment.

The fact is, ladies and gentlemen, the distance between this platform and the slave plantation, from which I escaped, is considerable and the difficulties to be overcome in getting from the latter to the former, are by no means slight. That I am here to-day is, to me, a matter of astonishment as well as of gratitude. You will not, therefore, be surprised, if in what I have to say. I evince no elaborate preparation, nor grace my speech with any high sounding exordium. With little experience and with less learning, I have been able to throw my thoughts hastily and imperfectly together; and trusting to your patient and generous indulgence, I will proceed to lay them before you.

This, for the purpose of this celebration, is the 4th of July. It is the birthday of your National Independence, and of your political freedom. This, to you, is what the Passover was to the emancipated people of God. It carries your minds back to the day, and to the act of your great deliverance; and to the signs, and to the wonders, associated with that act, and that day. This celebration also marks the beginning of another year of your national life; and reminds you that the Republic of America is now 76 years old. I am glad, fellow-citizens, that your nation is so young. Seventy-six years, though a good old age for a man, is but a mere speck in the life of a nation. Three score years and ten is the allotted time for individual men; but nations number their years by thousands. According to this fact, you are, even now, only in the beginning of your national career, still lingering in the period of childhood. I repeat, I am glad this is so. There is hope in the thought, and hope is much needed, under the dark clouds which lower above the horizon. The eye of the reformer is met with angry flashes, portending disastrous times; but his heart may well beat lighter at the thought that America is young, and that she is still in the impressible stage of her existence. May he not hope that high lessons of wisdom, of justice and of truth, will yet give direction to her destiny? Were the nation older, the patriot's heart might be sadder, and the reformer's brow heavier. Its future might be shrouded in gloom, and the hope of its prophets go out in sorrow. There is consolation in the thought that America is young. Great streams are not easily turned from channels, worn deep in the course of ages. They may sometimes rise in quiet and stately majesty, and inundate the land, refreshing and fertilizing the earth with their mysterious properties. They may also rise in wrath and fury, and bear away, on their angry waves, the accumulated wealth of years of toil and hardship. They, however, gradually flow back to the same old channel, and flow on as serenely as ever. But, while the river may not be turned aside, it may dry up, and leave nothing behind but the withered branch, and the unsightly rock, to howl in the abyss-sweeping wind, the sad tale of departed glory. As with rivers so with nations.

Fellow-citizens, I shall not presume to dwell at length on the associations that cluster about this day. The simple story of it is that, 76 years ago, the people of this country were British subjects. The style and title of your "sovereign people" (in which you now glory) was not then born. You were under the British Crown. Your fathers esteemed the English Government as the home government; and England as the fatherland. This home government, you know, although a considerable distance from your home, did, in the exercise of its parental prerogatives, impose upon its colonial children, such restraints, burdens and limitations, as, in its mature judgment, it deemed wise, right and proper.

But, your fathers, who had not adopted the fashionable idea of this day, of the infallibility of government, and the absolute character of its acts, presumed to differ from the home government in respect to the wisdom and the justice of some of those burdens and restraints. They went so far in their excitement as to pronounce the measures of government unjust, unreasonable, and oppressive, and altogether such as ought not to be quietly submitted to. I scarcely need say, fellow-citizens, that my opinion of those measures fully accords with that of your fathers. Such a declaration of agreement on my part would not be worth much to anybody. It would, certainly, prove nothing, as to what part I might have taken, had I lived during the great controversy of 1776. To say now that America was right, and England wrong, is exceedingly easy. Everybody can say it; the dastard, not less than the noble brave, can flippantly discant on the tyranny of England towards the American Colonies. It is fashionable to do so; but there was a time when to pronounce against England, and in favor of the cause of the colonies, tried men's souls. They who did so were accounted in their day, plotters of mischief, agitators and rebels, dangerous men. To side with the right, against the wrong, with the weak against the strong, and with the oppressed against the oppressor! here lies the merit, and the one which, of all others, seems unfashionable in our day. The cause of liberty may be stabbed by the men who glory in the deeds of your fathers. But, to proceed.

Feeling themselves harshly and unjustly treated by the home government, your fathers, like men of honesty, and men of spirit, earnestly sought redress. They petitioned and remonstrated; they did so in a decorous, respectful, and loyal manner. Their conduct was wholly unexceptionable. This, however, did not answer the purpose. They saw themselves treated with sovereign indifference, coldness and scorn. Yet they persevered. They were not the men to look back.

As the sheet anchor takes a firmer hold, when the ship is tossed by the storm, so did the cause of your fathers grow stronger, as it breasted the chilling blasts of kingly displeasure. The greatest and best of British statesmen admitted its justice, and the loftiest eloquence of the British Senate came to its support. But, with that blindness which seems to be the unvarying characteristic of tyrants, since Pharaoh and his hosts were drowned in the Red Sea, the British Government persisted in the exactions complained of.

The madness of this course, we believe, is admitted now, even by England; but we fear the lesson is wholly lost on our present ruler.

Oppression makes a wise man mad. Your fathers were wise men, and if they did not go mad, they became restive under this treatment. They felt themselves the victims of grievous wrongs, wholly incurable in their colonial capacity. With brave men there is always a remedy for oppression. Just here, the idea of a total separation of the colonies from the crown was born! It was a startling idea, much more so, than we, at this distance of time, regard it. The timid and the prudent (as has been intimated) of that day, were, of course, shocked and alarmed by it.

Such people lived then, had lived before, and will, probably, ever have a place on this planet; and their course, in respect to any great change, (no matter how great the good to be attained, or the wrong to be redressed by it), may be calculated with as much precision as can be the course of the stars. They hate all changes, but silver, gold and copper change! Of this sort of change they are always strongly in favor.

These people were called Tories in the days of your fathers; and the appellation, probably, conveyed the same idea that is meant by a more modern, though a somewhat less euphonious term, which we often find in our papers, applied to some of our old politicians.

Their opposition to the then dangerous thought was earnest and powerful; but, amid all their terror and affrighted vociferations against it, the alarming and revolutionary idea moved on, and the country with it.

On the 2d of July, 1776, the old Continental Congress, to the dismay of the lovers of ease, and the worshipers of property, clothed that dreadful idea with all the authority of national sanction. They did so in the form of a resolution; and as we seldom hit upon resolutions, drawn up in our day whose transparency is at all equal to this, it may refresh your minds and help my story if I read it. "Resolved, That these united colonies are, and of right, ought to be free and Independent States; that they are absolved from all allegiance to the British Crown; and that all political connection between them and the State of Great Britain is, and ought to be, dissolved."

Citizens, your fathers made good that resolution. They succeeded; and to-day you reap the fruits of their success. The freedom gained is yours; and you, therefore, may properly celebrate this anniversary. The 4th of July is the first great fact in your nation's history – the very ring-bolt in the chain of your yet undeveloped destiny.

Pride and patriotism, not less than gratitude, prompt you to celebrate and to hold it in perpetual remembrance. I have said that the Declaration of Independence is the ring-bolt to the chain of your nation's destiny; so, indeed, I regard it. The principles contained in that instrument are saving principles. Stand by those principles, be true to them on all occasions, in all places, against all foes, and at whatever cost.

From the round top of your ship of state, dark and threatening clouds may be seen. Heavy billows, like mountains in the distance, disclose to the leeward huge forms of flinty rocks! That bolt drawn, that chain broken, and all is lost. Cling to this day - cling to it, and to its principles, with the grasp of a storm-tossed mariner to a spar at midnight.

The coming into being of a nation, in any circumstances, is an interesting event. But, besides general considerations, there were peculiar circumstances which make the advent of this republic an event of special attractiveness.

The whole scene, as I look back to it, was simple, dignified and sublime.

The population of the country, at the time, stood at the insignificant number of three millions. The country was poor in the munitions of war. The population was weak and scattered, and the country a wilderness unsubdued. There were then no means of concert and combination, such as exist now. Neither steam nor lightning had then been reduced to order and discipline. From the Potomac to the Delaware was a journey of many days. Under these, and innumerable other disadvantages, your fathers declared for liberty and independence and triumphed.

Fellow Citizens, I am not wanting in respect for the fathers of this republic. The signers of the Declaration of Independence were brave men. They were great men too great enough to give fame to a great age. It does not often happen to a nation to raise, at one time, such a number of truly great men. The point from which I am compelled to view them is not, certainly, the most favorable; and yet I cannot contemplate their great deeds with less than admiration. They were statesmen, patriots and heroes, and for the good they did, and the principles they contended for, I will unite with you to honor their memory.

They loved their country better than their own private interests; and, though this is not the highest form of human excellence, all will concede that it is a rare virtue, and that when it is exhibited, it ought to command respect. He who will, intelligently, lay down his life for his country, is a man whom it is not in human nature to despise. Your fathers staked their lives, their fortunes, and their sacred honor, on the cause of their country. In their admiration of liberty, they lost sight of all other interests.

They were peace men; but they preferred revolution to peaceful submission to bondage. They were quiet men; but they did not shrink from agitating against oppression. They showed forbearance; but that they knew its limits. They believed in order; but not in the order of tyranny. With them, nothing was "settled" that was not right. With them, justice, liberty and humanity were "final;" not slavery and oppression. You may well cherish the memory of such men. They were great in their day and generation. Their solid manhood stands out the more as we contrast it with these degenerate times.

How circumspect, exact and proportionate were all their movements! How unlike the politicians of an hour! Their statesmanship looked beyond the passing moment, and stretched away in strength into the distant future. They seized upon eternal principles, and set a glorious example in their defense. Mark them!

Fully appreciating the hardship to be encountered, firmly believing in the right of their cause, honorably inviting the scrutiny of an on-looking world, reverently appealing to heaven to attest their sincerity, soundly comprehending the solemn responsibility they were about to assume, wisely measuring the terrible odds against them, your fathers, the fathers of this republic, did, most deliberately, under the inspiration of a glorious patriotism, and with a sublime faith in the great principles of justice and freedom, lay deep the corner-stone of the national superstructure, which has risen and still rises in grandeur around you.

Of this fundamental work, this day is the anniversary. Our eyes are met with demonstrations of joyous enthusiasm.

Banners and pennants wave exultingly on the breeze. The din of business, too, is hushed. Even Mammon seems to have quitted his grasp on this day. The ear-piercing fife and the stirring drum unite their accents with the ascending peal of a thousand church bells. Prayers are made, hymns are sung, and sermons are preached in honor of this day; while the quick martial tramp of a great and multitudinous nation, echoed back by all the hills, valleys and mountains of a vast continent, bespeak the occasion one of thrilling and universal interests nation's jubilee.

Friends and citizens, I need not enter further into the causes which led to this anniversary. Many of you understand them better than I do. You could instruct me in regard to them. That is a branch of knowledge in which you feel, perhaps, a much deeper interest than your speaker. The causes which led to the separation of the colonies from the British crown have never lacked for a tongue. They have all been taught in your common schools, narrated at your firesides, unfolded from your pulpits, and thundered from your legislative halls, and are as familiar to you as household words. They form the staple of your national poetry and eloquence.

I remember, also, that, as a people, Americans are remarkably familiar with all facts which make in their own favor. This is esteemed by some as a national trait - perhaps a national weakness. It is a fact, that whatever makes for the wealth or for the reputation of Americans, and can be had cheap! will be found by Americans. I shall not be charged with slandering Americans, if I say I think the American side of any question may be safely left in American hands.

I leave, therefore, the great deeds of your fathers to other gentlemen whose claim to have been regularly descended will be less likely to be disputed than mine!

THE PRESENT.

My business, if I have any here to-day, is with the present. The accepted time with God and his cause is the ever-living now.

> "Trust no future, however pleasant,
> Let the dead past bury its dead;
> Act, act in the living present,
> Heart within, and God overhead."

We have to do with the past only as we can make it useful to the present and to the future. To all inspiring motives, to noble deeds which can be gained from the past, we are welcome. But now is the time, the important time. Your fathers have lived, died, and have done their work, and have done much of it well. You live and must die, and you must do your work. You have no right to enjoy a child's share in the labor of your fathers, unless your children are to be blest by your labors. You have no right to wear out and waste the hard-earned fame of your fathers to cover your indolence. Sydney Smith tells us that men seldom eulogize the wisdom and virtues of their fathers, but to excuse some folly or wickedness of their own. This truth is not a doubtful one. There are illustrations of it near and remote, ancient and modern. It was fashionable, hundreds of years ago, for the children of Jacob to boast, we have "Abraham to our father," when they had long lost Abraham's faith and spirit. That people contented themselves under the shadow of Abraham's great name, while they repudiated the deeds which made his name great. Need I remind you that a similar thing is being done all over this country to-day? Need I tell you that the Jews are not the only people who built the tombs of the prophets, and garnished the sepulchres of the righteous? Washington could not die till he had broken the chains of his slaves. Yet his monument is built up by the price of human blood, and the traders in the bodies and souls of men, shout - "We have Washington to our father." Alas! that it should be so; yet so it is.

> "The evil that men do, lives after them,
> The good is oft' interred with their bones."

"What have I, or those I represent, to do with your national independence?"

Fellow-citizens, pardon me, allow me to ask, why am I called upon to speak here to-day? What have I, or those I represent, to do with your national independence? Are the great principles of political freedom and of natural justice, embodied in that Declaration of Independence, extended to us? and am I, therefore, called upon to bring our humble offering to the national altar, and to confess the benefits and express devout gratitude for the blessings resulting from your independence to us?

Would to God, both for your sakes and ours, that an affirmative answer could be truthfully returned to these questions! Then would my task be light, and my burden easy and delightful. For who is there so cold, that a nation's sympathy could not warm him? Who so obdurate and dead to the claims of gratitude, that would not thankfully acknowledge such priceless benefits? Who so stolid and selfish, that would not give his voice to swell the hallelujahs of a nation's jubilee, when the chains of servitude had been torn from his limbs? I am not that man. In a case like that, the dumb might eloquently speak, and the "lame man leap as an hart."

But, such is not the state of the case. I say it with a sad sense of the disparity between us. I am not included within the pale of this glorious anniversary! Your high independence only reveals the immeasurable distance between us. The blessings in which you, this day, rejoice, are not enjoyed in common. The rich inheritance of justice, liberty, prosperity and independence, bequeathed by your fathers, is shared by you, not by me. The sunlight that brought life and healing to you, has brought stripes and death to me. This Fourth [of] July is yours, not mine. You may rejoice, I must mourn. To drag a man in fetters into the grand illuminated temple of liberty, and call upon him to join you in joyous anthems, were inhuman mockery and sacrilegious irony. Do you mean, citizens, to mock me, by asking me to speak to-day? If so, there is a parallel to your conduct. And let me warn you that it is dangerous to copy the example of a nation whose crimes, lowering up to heaven, were thrown down by the breath of the Almighty, burying that nation in irrecoverable ruin! I can to-day take up the plaintive lament of a peeled and woe-smitten people!

"By the rivers of Babylon, there we sat down. Yea! we wept when we remembered Zion. We hanged our harps upon the willows in the midst thereof. For there, they that carried us away captive, required of us a song; and they who wasted us required of us mirth, saying, Sing us one of the songs of Zion. How can we sing the Lord's song in a strange land? If I forget thee, O Jerusalem, let my right hand forget her cunning. If I do not remember thee, let my tongue cleave to the roof of my mouth."

Fellow-citizens; above your national, tumultuous joy, I hear the mournful wail of millions! whose chains, heavy and grievous yesterday, are, to-day, rendered more intolerable by the jubilee shouts that reach them. If I do forget, if I do not faithfully remember those bleeding children of sorrow this day, "may my right hand forget her cunning, and may my tongue cleave to the roof of my mouth!" To forget them, to pass lightly over their wrongs, and to chime in with the popular theme, would be treason most scandalous and shocking, and would make me a reproach before God and the world. My subject, then fellow-citizens, is American slavery. I shall see, this day, and its popular characteristics, from the slave's point of view. Standing, there, identified with the American bondman, making his wrongs mine, I do not hesitate to declare, with all my soul, that the character and conduct of this nation never looked blacker to me than on this 4th of July! Whether we turn to the declarations of the past, or to the professions of the present, the conduct of the nation seems equally hideous and revolting. America is false to the past, false to the present, and solemnly binds herself to be false to the future. Standing with God and the crushed and bleeding slave on this occasion, I will, in the name of humanity which is outraged, in the name of liberty which is fettered, in the name of the constitution and the Bible, which are disregarded and trampled upon, dare to call in question and to denounce, with all the emphasis I can command, everything that serves to perpetuate slavery-the great sin and shame of America! "I will not equivocate; I will not excuse;" I will use the severest language I can command; and yet not one word shall escape me that any man, whose judgment is not blinded by prejudice, or who is not at heart a slaveholder, shall not confess to be right and just.

But I fancy I hear some one of my audience say, it is just in this circumstance that you and your brother abolitionists fail to make a favorable impression on the public mind. Would you argue more, and denounce less, would you persuade more, and rebuke less, your cause would be much more likely to succeed. But, I submit, where all is plain there is nothing to be argued. What point in the anti-slavery creed would you have me argue? On what branch of the subject do the people of this country need light? Must I undertake to prove that the slave is a man? That point is conceded already. Nobody doubts it. The slaveholders themselves acknowledge it in the enactment of laws for their government. They acknowledge it when they punish disobedience on the part of the slave. There are seventy-two crimes in the State of Virginia, which, if committed by a black man, (no matter how ignorant he be), subject him to the punishment of death; while only two of the same crimes will subject a white man to the like punishment. What is this but the acknowledgement that the slave is a moral, intellectual and responsible being? The manhood of the slave is conceded. It is admitted in the fact that Southern statute books are covered with enactments forbidding, under severe fines and penalties, the teaching of the slave to read or to write. When you can point to any such laws, in reference to the beasts of the field, then I may consent to argue the manhood of the slave. When the dogs in your streets, when the fowls of the air, when the cattle on your hills, when the fish of the sea, and the reptiles that crawl, shall be unable to distinguish the slave from a brute, their will I argue with you that the slave is a man!

For the present, it is enough to affirm the equal manhood of the Negro race. Is it not astonishing that, while we are ploughing, planting and reaping, using all kinds of mechanical tools, erecting houses, constructing bridges, building ships, working in metals of brass, iron, copper, silver and gold; that, while we are reading, writing and cyphering, acting as clerks, merchants and secretaries, having among us lawyers, doctors, ministers, poets, authors, editors, orators and teachers; that, while we are engaged in all manner of enterprises common to other men, digging gold in California, capturing the whale in the Pacific, feeding sheep and cattle on the hill-side, living, moving, acting, thinking, planning, living in families as husbands, wives and children, and, above all, confessing and worshipping the Christian's God, and looking hopefully for life and immortality beyond the grave, we are called upon to prove that we are men!

Would you have me argue that man is entitled to liberty? that he is the rightful owner of his own body? You have already declared it. Must I argue the wrongfulness of slavery? Is that a question for Republicans? Is it to be settled by the rules of logic and argumentation, as a matter beset with great difficulty, involving a doubtful application of the principle of justice, hard to be understood? How should I look to-day, in the presence of Americans, dividing, and subdividing a discourse, to show that men have a natural right to freedom? speaking of it relatively, and positively, negatively, and affirmatively. To do so, would be to make myself ridiculous, and to offer an insult to your understanding. There is not a man beneath the canopy of heaven, that does not know that slavery is wrong for him.

What, am I to argue that it is wrong to make men brutes, to rob them of their liberty, to work them without wages, to keep them ignorant of their relations to their fellow men, to beat them with sticks, to flay their flesh with the lash, to load their limbs with irons, to hunt them with dogs, to sell them at auction, to sunder their families, to knock out their teeth, to bum their flesh, to starve them into obedience and submission to their masters? Must I argue that a system thus marked with blood, and stained with pollution, is wrong? No! I will not. I have better employments for my time and strength than such arguments would imply.

What, then, remains to be argued? Is it that slavery is not divine; that God did not establish it; that our doctors of divinity are mistaken? There is blasphemy in the thought. That which is inhuman, cannot be divine! Who can reason on such a proposition? They that can, may; I cannot. The time for such argument is past.

At a time like this, scorching irony, not convincing argument, is needed. O! had I the ability, and could I reach the nation's ear, I would, to-day, pour out a fiery stream of biting ridicule, blasting reproach, withering sarcasm, and stern rebuke. For it is not light that is needed, but fire; it is not the gentle shower, but thunder. We need the storm, the whirlwind, and the earthquake. The feeling of the nation must be quickened; the conscience of the nation must be roused; the propriety of the nation must be startled; the hypocrisy of the nation must be exposed; and its crimes against God and man must be proclaimed and denounced.

What, to the American slave, is your 4th of July? I answer: a day that reveals to him, more than all other days in the year, the gross injustice and cruelly to which he is the constant victim. To him, your celebration is a sham; your boasted liberty, an unholy license; your national greatness, swelling vanity; your sounds of rejoicing are empty and heartless; your denunciations of tyrants, brass fronted impudence; your shouts of liberty and equality, hollow mockery; your prayers and hymns, your sermons and thanksgivings, with all your religious parade, and solemnity, are, to him, mere bombast, fraud, deception, impiety, and hypocrisy - a thin veil to cover up crimes which would disgrace a nation of savages. There is not a nation on the earth guilty of practices, more shocking and bloody, than are the people of these United States, at this very hour.

Go where you may, search where you will, roam through all the monarchies and despotisms of the old world, travel through South America, search out every abuse, and when you have found the last, lay your facts by the side of the everyday practices of this nation, and you will say with me, that, for revolting barbarity and shameless hypocrisy, America reigns without a rival.

INTERNAL SLAVE TRADE.

Take the American slave-trade, which, we are told by the papers, is especially prosperous just now. Ex-Senator Benton tells us that the price of men was never higher than now. He mentions the fact to show that slavery is in no danger. This trade is one of the peculiarities of American institutions. It is carried on in all the large towns and cities in one-half of this confederacy; and millions are pocketed every year, by dealers in this horrid traffic. In several states, this trade is a chief source of wealth. It is called (in contradistinction to the foreign slave-trade) "the internal slave trade." It is, probably, called so, too, in order to divert from it the horror with which the foreign slave-trade is contemplated. That trade has long since been denounced by this government, as piracy. It has been denounced with burning words, from the high places of the nation, as an execrable traffic. To arrest it, to put an end to it, this nation keeps a squadron, at immense cost, on the coast of Africa. Everywhere, in this country, it is safe to speak of this foreign slave-trade, as a most inhuman traffic, opposed alike to the laws of God and of man. The duty to extirpate and destroy it, is admitted even by our Doctors of Divinity. In order to put an end to it, some of these last have consented that their colored brethren (nominally free) should leave this country, and establish themselves on the western coast of Africa! It is, however, a notable fact that, while so much execration is poured out by Americans upon those engaged in the foreign slave-trade, the men engaged in the slave-trade between the states pass without condemnation, and their business is deemed honorable.

Behold the practical operation of this internal slave-trade, the American slave-trade, sustained by American politics and America religion. Here you will see men and women reared like swine for the market. You know what is a swine-drover? I will show you a man-drover. They inhabit all our Southern States. They perambulate the country, and crowd the highways of the nation, with droves of human stock. You will see one of these human flesh-jobbers, armed with pistol, whip and bowie-knife, driving a company of a hundred men, women, and children, from the Potomac to the slave market at New Orleans. These wretched people are to be sold singly, or in lots, to suit purchasers. They are food for the cotton-field, and the deadly sugar-mill. Mark the sad procession, as it moves wearily along, and the inhuman wretch who drives them. Hear his savage yells and his blood-chilling oaths, as he hurries on his affrighted captives! There, see the old man, with locks thinned and gray. Cast one glance, if you please, upon that young mother, whose shoulders are bare to the scorching sun, her briny tears falling on the brow of the babe in her arms. See, too, that girl of thirteen, weeping, yes! weeping, as she thinks of the mother from whom she has been torn! The drove moves tardily. Heat and sorrow have nearly consumed their strength; suddenly you hear a quick snap, like the discharge of a rifle; the fetters clank, and the chain rattles simultaneously; your ears are saluted with a scream, that seems to have torn its way to the center of your soul! The crack you heard, was the sound of the slave-whip; the scream you heard, was from the woman you saw with the babe. Her speed had faltered under the weight of her child and her chains! that gash on her shoulder tells her to move on. Follow the drove to New Orleans. Attend the auction; see men examined like horses; see the forms of women rudely and brutally exposed to the shocking gaze of American slave-buyers. See this drove sold and separated forever; and never forget the deep, sad sobs that arose from that scattered multitude. Tell me citizens, where, under the sun, you can witness a spectacle more fiendish and shocking. Yet this is but a glance at the American slave-trade, as it exists, at this moment, in the ruling part of the United States.

I was born amid such sights and scenes. To me the American slave-trade is a terrible reality. When a child, my soul was often pierced with a sense of its horrors. I lived on Philpot Street, Fell's Point, Baltimore, and have watched from the wharves, the slave ships in the Basin, anchored from the shore, with their cargoes of human flesh, waiting for favorable winds to waft them down the Chesapeake. There was, at that time, a grand slave mart kept at the head of Pratt Street, by Austin Woldfolk. His agents were sent into every town and county in Maryland, announcing their arrival, through the papers, and on flaming "hand-bills," headed CASH FOR NEGROES. These men were generally well dressed men, and very captivating in their manners. Ever ready to drink, to treat, and to gamble. The fate of many a slave has depended upon the turn of a single card; and many a child has been snatched from the arms of its mother by bargains arranged in a state of brutal drunkenness.

The flesh-mongers gather up their victims by dozens, and drive them, chained, to the general depot at Baltimore. When a sufficient number have been collected here, a ship is chartered, for the purpose of conveying the forlorn crew to Mobile, or to New Orleans. From the slave prison to the ship, they are usually driven in the darkness of night; for since the antislavery agitation, a certain caution is observed.

In the deep still darkness of midnight, I have been often aroused by the dead heavy footsteps, and the piteous cries of the chained gangs that passed our door. The anguish of my boyish heart was intense; and I was often consoled, when speaking to my mistress in the morning, to hear her say that the custom was very wicked; that she hated to hear the rattle of the chains, and the heart-rending cries. I was glad to find one who sympathized with me in my horror.

Fellow-citizens, this murderous traffic is, to-day, in active operation in this boasted republic. In the solitude of my spirit, I see clouds of dust raised on the highways of the South; I see the bleeding footsteps; I hear the doleful wail of fettered humanity, on the way to the slave-markets, where the victims are to be sold like horses, sheep, and swine, knocked off to the highest bidder. There I see the tenderest ties ruthlessly broken, to gratify the lust, caprice and rapacity of the buyers and sellers of men. My soul sickens at the sight.

> "Is this the land your Fathers loved,
> The freedom which they toiled to win?
> Is this the earth whereon they moved?
> Are these the graves they slumber in?"

But a still more inhuman, disgraceful, and scandalous state of things remains to be presented.

By an act of the American Congress, not yet two years old, slavery has been nationalized in its most horrible and revolting form. By that act, Mason & Dixon's line has been obliterated; New York has become as Virginia; and the power to hold, hunt, and sell men, women, and children as slaves remains no longer a mere state institution, but is now an institution of the whole United States. The power is co-extensive with the Star-Spangled Banner and American Christianity. Where these go, may also go the merciless slave-hunter. Where these are, man is not sacred. He is a bird for the sportsman's gun. By that most foul and fiendish of all human decrees, the liberty and person of every man are put in peril. Your broad republican domain is hunting ground for men. Not for thieves and robbers, enemies of society, merely, but for men guilty of no crime. Your lawmakers have commanded all good citizens to engage in this hellish sport. Your President, your Secretary of State, your lords, nobles, and ecclesiastics, enforce, as a duty you owe to your free and glorious country, and to your God, that you do this accursed thing. Not fewer than forty Americans have, within the past two years, been hunted down and, without a moment's warning, hurried away in chains, and consigned to slavery and excruciating torture. Some of these have had wives and children, dependent on them for bread; but of this, no account was made. The right of the hunter to his prey stands superior to the right of marriage, and to all rights in this republic, the rights of God included! For black men there are neither law, justice, humanity, not religion. The Fugitive Slave Law makes mercy to them a crime; and bribes the judge who tries them. An American judge gets ten dollars for every victim he consigns to slavery, and five, when he fails to do so. The oath of any two villains is sufficient, under this hell-black enactment, to send the most pious and exemplary black man into the remorseless jaws of slavery! His own testimony is nothing. He can bring no witnesses for himself. The minister of American justice is bound by the law to hear but one side; and that side, is the side of the oppressor. Let this damning fact be perpetually told. Let it be thundered around the world, that, in tyrant-killing, king-hating, people-loving, democratic, Christian America, the seats of justice are filled with judges, who hold their offices under an open and palpable bribe, and are bound, in deciding in the case of a man's liberty, hear only his accusers!

In glaring violation of justice, in shameless disregard of the forms of administering law, in cunning arrangement to entrap the defenseless, and in diabolical intent, this Fugitive Slave Law stands alone in the annals of tyrannical legislation. I doubt if there be another nation on the globe, having the brass and the baseness to put such a law on the statute-book. If any man in this assembly thinks differently from me in this matter, and feels able to disprove my statements, I will gladly confront him at any suitable time and place he may select.

RELIGIOUS LIBERTY.

I take this law to be one of the grossest infringements of Christian Liberty, and, if the churches and ministers of our country were not stupidly blind, or most wickedly indifferent, they, too, would so regard it.

At the very moment that they are thanking God for the enjoyment of civil and religious liberty, and for the right to worship God according to the dictates of their own consciences, they are utterly silent in respect to a law which robs religion of its chief significance, and makes it utterly worthless to a world lying in wickedness. Did this law concern the "mint, anise and cummin" abridge the fight to sing psalms, to partake of the sacrament, or to engage in any of the ceremonies of religion, it would be smitten by the thunder of a thousand pulpits. A general shout would go up from the church, demanding repeal, repeal, instant repeal! And it would go hard with that politician who presumed to solicit the votes of the people without inscribing this motto on his banner. Further, if this demand were not complied with, another Scotland would be added to the history of religious liberty, and the stern old Covenanters would be thrown into the shade. A John Knox would be seen at every church door, and heard from every pulpit, and Fillmore would have no more quarter than was shown by Knox, to the beautiful, but treacherous queen Mary of Scotland. The fact that the church of our country, (with fractional exceptions), does not esteem "the Fugitive Slave Law" as a declaration of war against religious liberty, implies that that church regards religion simply as a form of worship, an empty ceremony, and not a vital principle, requiring active benevolence, justice, love and good will towards man. It esteems sacrifice above mercy; psalm-singing above right doing; solemn meetings above practical righteousness. A worship that can be conducted by persons who refuse to give shelter to the houseless, to give bread to the hungry, clothing to the naked, and who enjoin obedience to a law forbidding these acts of mercy, is a curse, not a blessing to mankind. The Bible addresses all such persons as "scribes, Pharisees, hypocrites, who pay tithe of mint, anise, and cummin, and have omitted the weightier matters of the law, judgment, mercy and faith."

THE CHURCH RESPONSIBLE.

But the church of this country is not only indifferent to the wrongs of the slave, it actually takes sides with the oppressors. It has made itself the bulwark of American slavery, and the shield of American slave-hunters. Many of its most eloquent Divines who stand as the very lights of the church, have shamelessly given the sanction of religion and the Bible to the whole slave system. They have taught that man may, properly, be a slave; that the relation of master and slave is ordained of God; that to send back an escaped bondman to his master is clearly the duty of all the followers of the Lord Jesus Christ; and this horrible blasphemy is palmed off upon the world for Christianity.

For my part, I would say, welcome infidelity! welcome atheism! Welcome anything! in preference to the gospel, as preached by those Divines! They convert the very name of religion into an engine of tyranny, and barbarous cruelty, and serve to confirm more infidels, in this age, than all the infidel writings of Thomas Paine, Voltaire, and Bolingbroke, put together, have done! These ministers make religion a cold and flinty-hearted thing, having neither principles of right action, nor bowels of compassion. They strip the love of God of its beauty, and leave the throng of religion a huge, horrible, repulsive form. It is a religion for oppressors, tyrants, man-stealers, and thugs. It is not that "pure and undefiled religion" which is from above, and which is "first pure, then peaceable, easy to be entreated, full of mercy and good fruits, without partiality, and without hypocrisy." But a religion which favors the rich against the poor; which exalts the proud above the humble; which divides mankind into two classes, tyrants and slaves; which says to the man in chains, stay there; and to the oppressor, oppress on; it is a religion which may be professed and enjoyed by all the robbers and enslavers of mankind; it makes God a respecter of persons, denies his fatherhood of the race, and tramples in the dust the great truth of the brotherhood of man. All this we affirm to be true of the popular church, and the popular worship of our land and nation - a religion, a church, and a worship which, on the authority of inspired wisdom, we pronounce to be an abomination in the sight of God. In the language of Isaiah, the American church might be well addressed, "Bring no more vain ablations; incense is an abomination unto me: the new moons and Sabbaths, the calling of assemblies, I cannot away with; it is iniquity even the solemn meeting.

Your new moons and your appointed feasts my soul hateth. They are a trouble to me; I am weary to bear them; and when ye spread forth your hands I will hide mine eyes from you. Yea! when ye make many prayers, I will not hear. YOUR HANDS ARE FULL OF BLOOD; cease to do evil, learn to do well; seek judgment; relieve the oppressed; judge for the fatherless; plead for the widow."

The American church is guilty, when viewed in connection with what it is doing to uphold slavery; but it is superlatively guilty when viewed in connection with its ability to abolish slavery. The sin of which it is guilty is one of omission as well as of commission. Albert Barnes but uttered what the common sense of every man at all observant of the actual state of the case will receive as truth, when he declared that "There is no power out of the church that could sustain slavery an hour, if it were not sustained in it."

Let the religious press, the pulpit, the Sunday school, the conference meeting, the great ecclesiastical, missionary, Bible and tract associations of the land array their immense powers against slavery and slave-holding; and the whole system of crime and blood would be scattered to the winds; and that they do not do this involves them in the most awful responsibility of which the mind can conceive.

In prosecuting the anti-slavery enterprise, we have been asked to spare the church, to spare the ministry; but how, we ask, could such a thing be done? We are met on the threshold of our efforts for the redemption of the slave, by the church and ministry of the country, in battle arrayed against us; and we are compelled to fight or flee. From what quarter, I beg to know, has proceeded a fire so deadly upon our ranks, during the last two years, as from the Northern pulpit? As the champions of oppressors, the chosen men of American theology have appeared-men, honored for their so-called piety, and their real learning. The Lords of Buffalo, the Springsof New York, the Lathrops of Auburn, the Coxes and Spensors of Brooklyn, the Gannets and Sharps of Boston, the Deweys of Washington, and other great religious lights of the land, have, in utter denial of the authority of Him, by whom the professed to he called to the ministry, deliberately taught us, against the example or the Hebrews and against the remonstrance of the Apostles, they teach "that we ought to obey man's law before the law of God."

My spirit wearies of such blasphemy; and how such men can be supported, as the "standing types and representatives of Jesus Christ," is a mystery which I leave others to penetrate. In speaking of the American church, however, let it be distinctly understood that I mean the great mass of the religious organizations of our land. There are exceptions, and I thank God that there are. Noble men may be found, scattered all over these Northern States, of whom Henry Ward Beecher of Brooklyn, Samuel J. May of Syracuse, and my esteemed friend on the platform, are shining examples; and let me say further, that upon these men lies the duty to inspire our ranks with high religious faith and zeal, and to cheer us on in the great mission of the slave's redemption from his chains.

RELIGION IN ENGLAND AND
RELIGION IN AMERICA.

One is struck with the difference between the attitude of the American church towards the anti-slavery movement, and that occupied by the churches in England towards a similar movement in that country. There, the church, true to its mission of ameliorating, elevating, and improving the condition of mankind, came forward promptly, bound up the wounds of the West Indian slave, and restored him to his liberty. There, the question of emancipation was a high[ly] religious question. It was demanded, in the name of humanity, and according to the law of the living God. The Sharps, the Clarksons, the Wilberforces, the Buxtons, and Burchells and the Knibbs, were alike famous for their piety, and for their philanthropy. The anti-slavery movement there was not an anti-church movement, for the reason that the church took its full share in prosecuting that movement: and the anti-slavery movement in this country will cease to be an anti-church movement, when the church of this country shall assume a favorable, instead or a hostile position towards that movement. Americans! your republican politics, not less than your republican religion, are flagrantly inconsistent. You boast of your love of liberty, your superior civilization, and your pure Christianity, while the whole political power of the nation (as embodied in the two great political parties), is solemnly pledged to support and perpetuate the enslavement of three millions of your countrymen. You hurl your anathemas at the crowned headed tyrants of Russia and Austria, and pride yourselves on your Democratic institutions, while you yourselves consent to be the mere tools and bodyguards of the tyrants of Virginia and Carolina. You invite to your shores fugitives of oppression from abroad, honor them with banquets, greet them with ovations, cheer them, toast them, salute them, protect them, and pour out your money to them like water; but the fugitives from your own land you advertise, hunt, arrest, shoot and kill. You glory in your refinement and your universal education yet you maintain a system as barbarous and dreadful as ever stained the character of a nation - a system begun in avarice, supported in pride, and perpetuated in cruelty. You shed tears over fallen Hungary, and make the sad story of her wrongs the theme of your poets, statesmen and orators, till your gallant sons are ready to fly to arms to vindicate her cause against her oppressors; but, in regard to the ten thousand wrongs of the American slave, you would enforce the strictest silence, and would hail him as an enemy of the nation who dares to make those wrongs the subject of public discourse! You are all on fire at the mention of liberty for France or for Ireland; but are as cold as an iceberg at the thought of liberty for the enslaved of America. You discourse eloquently on the dignity of labor; yet, you sustain a system which, in its very essence, casts a stigma upon labor. You can bare your bosom to the storm of British artillery to throw off a threepenny tax on tea; and yet wring the last hard-earned farthing from the grasp of the black laborers of your country. You profess to believe "that, of one blood, God made all nations of men to dwell on the face of all the earth," and hath commanded all men, everywhere to love one another; yet you notoriously hate, (and glory in your hatred), all men whose skins are not colored like your own. You declare, before the world, and are understood by the world to declare, that you "hotel these truths to be self evident, that all men are created equal; and are endowed by their Creator with certain inalienable rights; and that, among these are, life, liberty, and the pursuit of happiness;" and yet, you hold securely, in a bondage which, according to your own Thomas Jefferson, "is worse than ages of that which your fathers rose in rebellion to oppose," a seventh part of the inhabitants of your country.

Fellow-citizens! I will not enlarge further on your national inconsistencies. The existence of slavery in this country brands your republicanism as a sham, your humanity as a base pretence, and your Christianity as a lie. It destroys your moral power abroad; it corrupts your politicians at home. It saps the foundation of religion; it makes your name a hissing, and a by word to a mocking earth. It is the antagonistic force in your government, the only thing that seriously disturbs and endangers your Union. It fetters your progress; it is the enemy of improvement, the deadly foe of education; it fosters pride; it breeds insolence; it promotes vice; it shelters crime; it is a curse to the earth that supports it; and yet, you cling to it, as if it were the sheet anchor of all your hopes. Oh! be warned! be warned! a horrible reptile is coiled up in your nation's bosom; the venomous creature is nursing at the tender breast of your youthful republic; for the love of God, tear away, and fling from you the hideous monster, and let the weight of twenty millions crush and destroy it forever!

THE CONSTITUTION.

But it is answered in reply to all this, that precisely what I have now denounced is, in fact, guaranteed and sanctioned by the Constitution of the United States; that the right to hold and to hunt slaves is a part of that Constitution framed by the illustrious Fathers of this Republic.

Then, I dare to affirm, notwithstanding all I have said before, your fathers stooped, basely stooped "To palter with us in a double sense: And keep the word of promise to the ear, But break it to the heart."

And instead of being the honest men I have before declared them to be, they were the veriest imposters that ever practiced on mankind. This is the inevitable conclusion, and from it there is no escape. But I differ from those who charge this baseness on the framers of the Constitution of the United States. It is a slander upon their memory, at least, so I believe. There is not time now to argue the constitutional question at length - nor have I the ability to discuss it as it ought to be discussed. The subject has been handled with masterly power by Lysander Spooner, Esq., by William Goodell, by Samuel E. Sewall, Esq., and last, though not least, by Gerritt Smith, Esq. These gentlemen have, as I think, fully and clearly vindicated the Constitution from any design to support slavery for an hour.

"[L]et me ask, if it be not somewhat singular that, if the Constitution were intended to be, by its framers and adopters, a slave-holding instrument, why neither slavery, slaveholding, nor slave can anywhere be found in it."

Fellow-citizens! there is no matter in respect to which, the people of the North have allowed themselves to be so ruinously imposed upon, as that of the pro-slavery character of the Constitution. In that instrument I hold there is neither warrant, license, nor sanction of the hateful thing; but, interpreted as it ought to be interpreted, the Constitution is a GLORIOUS LIBERTY DOCUMENT. Read its preamble, consider its purposes. Is slavery among them? Is it at the gateway? or is it in the temple? It is neither. While I do not intend to argue this question on the present occasion, let me ask, if it be not somewhat singular that, if the Constitution were intended to be, by its framers and adopters, a slave-holding instrument, why neither slavery, slaveholding, nor slave can anywhere be found in it. What would be thought of an instrument, drawn up, legally drawn up, for the purpose of entitling the city of Rochester to a track of land, in which no mention of land was made? Now, there are certain rules of interpretation, for the proper understanding of all legal instruments. These rules are well established. They are plain, common-sense rules, such as you and I, and all of us, can understand and apply, without having passed years in the study of law. I scout the idea that the question of the constitutionality or unconstitutionality of slavery is not a question for the people. I hold that every American citizen has a fight to form an opinion of the constitution, and to propagate that opinion, and to use all honorable means to make his opinion the prevailing one. Without this fight, the liberty of an American citizen would be as insecure as that of a Frenchman. Ex-Vice-President Dallas tells us that the constitution is an object to which no American mind can be too attentive, and no American heart too devoted. He further says, the constitution, in its words, is plain and intelligible, and is meant for the home-bred, unsophisticated understandings of our fellow-citizens. Senator Berrien tell us that the Constitution is the fundamental law, that which controls all others. The charter of our liberties, which every citizen has a personal interest in understanding thoroughly. The testimony of Senator Breese, Lewis Cass, and many others that might be named, who are everywhere esteemed as sound lawyers, so regard the constitution. I take it, therefore, that it is not presumption in a private citizen to form an opinion of that instrument.

Now, take the constitution according to its plain reading, and I defy the presentation of a single pro-slavery clause in it. On the other hand it will be found to contain principles and purposes, entirely hostile to the existence of slavery.

I have detained my audience entirely too long already. At some future period I will gladly avail myself of an opportunity to give this subject a full and fair discussion.

"Allow me to say, in conclusion, notwithstanding the dark picture I have this day presented of the state of the nation, I do not despair of this country."

There are forces in operation, which must inevitably work the downfall of slavery. "The arm of the Lord is not shortened," and the doom of slavery is certain. I, therefore, leave off where I began, with hope. While drawing encouragement from the Declaration of Independence, the great principles it contains, and the genius of American Institutions, my spirit is also cheered by the obvious tendencies of the age. Nations do not now stand in the same relation to each other that they did ages ago. No nation can now shut itself up from the surrounding world, and trot round in the same old path of its fathers without interference. The time was when such could be done. Long established customs of hurtful character could formerly fence themselves in, and do their evil work with social impunity. Knowledge was then confined and enjoyed by the privileged few, and the multitude walked on in mental darkness. But a change has now come over the affairs of mankind. Walled cities and empires have become unfashionable. The arm of commerce has borne away the gates of the strong city. Intelligence is penetrating the darkest corners of the globe. It makes its pathway over and under the sea, as well as on the earth. Wind, steam, and lightning are its chartered agents. Oceans no longer divide, but link nations together. From Boston to London is now a holiday excursion. Space is comparatively annihilated. Thoughts expressed on one side of the Atlantic are, distinctly heard on the other. The far off and almost fabulous Pacific rolls in grandeur at our feet. The Celestial Empire, the mystery of ages, is being solved. The fiat of the Almighty, "Let there be Light," has not yet spent its force. No abuse, no outrage whether in taste, sport or avarice, can now hide itself from the all-pervading light. The iron shoe, and crippled foot of China must be seen, in contrast with nature. Africa must rise and put on her yet unwoven garment. "Ethiopia shall stretch out her hand unto God." In the fervent aspirations of William Lloyd Garrison, I say, and let every heart join in saying it:

God speed the year of jubilee
The wide world over
When from their galling chains set free,
The oppressed shall vilely bend the knee,
And wear the yoke of tyranny
Like brutes no more.

That year will come, and freedom's reign,
To man his plundered fights again
            Restore.

God speed the day when human blood
        Shall cease to flow!
In every clime be understood,
The claims of human brotherhood,
And each return for evil, good,
        Not blow for blow;
That day will come all feuds to end.
And change into a faithful friend
        Each foe.

God speed the hour, the glorious hour,
        When none on earth
Shall exercise a lordly power,
Nor in a tyrant's presence cower;
But all to manhood's stature tower,
        By equal birth!
THAT HOUR WILL, COME, to each, to all,
And from his prison-house, the thrall
        Go forth.

Until that year, day, hour, arrive,
With head, and heart, and hand I'll strive,
To break the rod, and rend the gyve,
The spoiler of his prey deprive-
        So witness Heaven!
And never from my chosen post,
Whatever the peril or the cost,
        Be driven.

A PORTION OF PROCEEDS FROM THE SALE OF THIS BOOK GO TO:

The Frederick Douglass-Isaac Myers
Maritime Park

Created as a Living Classrooms Facility in Baltimore, the Maritime Park is built on the exact site of Douglass' apprenticeship as a caulker in a shipyard before escaping from slavery. The site offers hands-on history lessons and seeks to become a significant African-American heritage site in the United States.

To find out more about the project, please go to
douglassmyers.org
or
call 410.685.0295.

www.ingramcontent.com/pod-product-compliance
Lightning Source LLC
Chambersburg PA
CBHW021048090426
42738CB00006B/247